The World Joke Book

OTHER WORKS BY ROBERT MULLER:

Most of All, They Taught Me Happiness (Amity House)

New Genesis, Shaping a Global Spirituality (Doubleday)

What War Taught Me About Peace (Amity House)

A Planet of Hope (Amity House)

Sima, Mon Amour, a French novel (Pierron)

The Desire to Be Human, edited by Robert Muller and Leo Zonneveld, an international compendium in honour of Teilhard de Chardin (Mirananda)

Decide to. . . (Acorn)

ABOUT THE AUTHOR:

Global Spirituality, Planetary Consciousness in the Thought of Teilhard de Chardin and Robert Muller, by Margaret McGurn

Robert Muller, Sopratutto Mi Insegnarono la Felicita, by Alessandro Carletti

Hacia El Planeta di Dios, Dialogos con Robert Muller, by Hilda Berger

The World Core Curriculum in the Robert Muller Elementary School, by Gloria Crook.

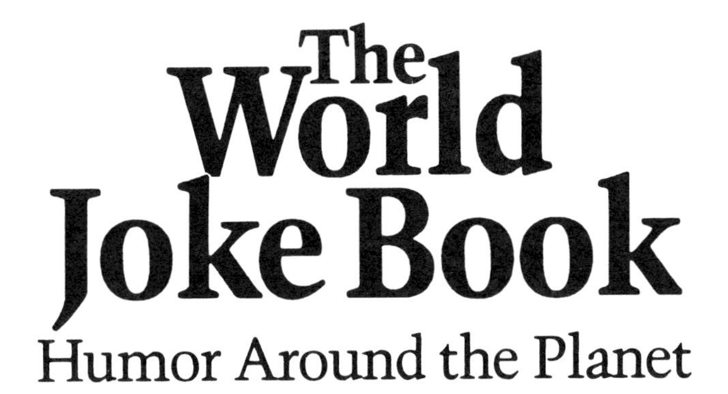

Robert Muller

AMITY HOUSE
AMITY, NEW YORK

Published by Amity House, Inc.
16 High Street
Warwick, N.Y. 10990

ISBN: 0-916349-42-X

Library of Congress Catalog Number 87-72999

I dedicate this book to the International Year of Peace, 1986, proclaimed by the United Nations. It is infinitely better for people and nations to laugh together than to fight each other.

Robert Muller
Assistant Secretary-General
United Nations

TABLE OF CONTENTS

FOREWORD

Deeply impressed by my friend Norman Cousins' story of how he healed himself of a severe sickness through laughter (*Anatomy of an Illness*, Norton, 1980), I devoted a chapter in my own book *Most of All, They Taught Me Happiness*, to humour being a means to deflate tension in international affairs.

Indeed, laughter, that extraordinary physiological and psychological phenomenon which shakes the entire body, is a major means of "communication" between human beings. Often at the United Nations, in meetings, at diplomatic negotiations, talks, receptions or dinners, I could see tensions mount dangerously — without any chance of return to normalcy through rational means. Yet, appropriate jokes (humour at the right moment) trigger a spark in the electrical current between highly charged poles, allowing defusion and a return to normal. Too little attention has been paid to humour in a world where practically everything is studied from the inside out. Only in recent years have scattered efforts by psychologists, psychiatrists and other disciplines begun to converge, resulting in a series of international conferences on humour — held successively in Wales, Los Angeles, Washington and Tel Aviv.

Think for a moment about the role of humour in our

world's cultural development. The fact that the same jokes can be found today in the most far-apart countries reveals an important cultural common denominator which might teach us a lot about the ways of the human race. Also, the fact that old jokes now reappear in international relations and that entirely new "world jokes" are being coined, indicates that world affairs are becoming part of the daily consciousness of people. There exists today a United Nations and thirty-two world agencies which deal with practically every problem under the sun, from nuclear proliferation to peace, from world population to individual human rights, from astrophysics to the atom. Despite all their frailties and growing pains, these unprecedented young agencies are humanity's best hope for peace and a better world. It is, therefore, reassuring that humour should have come of age in world affairs and in international institutions as an antidote for abusive power, vain glory, arrogance, untruth, intolerance, violation of human rights, discrimination and all other protracted evils which still beset the human race. I hope that someday, when our planet is a peaceful and happy celestial body in the universe, we will also be known as the Planet of Good Humour.

No harm or insult is meant to any person, group, institution, race, nation, culture, philosophy, religion, company or ideology in this collection of stories and jokes — conceived by people from all around the planet. Hence, this book has no real author, for each story has its unknown, forgotten or anonymous author. But, after a lifetime spent in humanity's first and fascinating universal organization, I want to share the jokes and humourous stories I have heard during my 38 years of world service with the United Nations. My sole purpose is to contribute to reading enjoyment, international understanding, contribute to a happier, healthier, more joyful world. I am pleased to make this contribution to the first International Year of Peace proclaimed on this Earth. Think how marvelous it is that in the vast, unfathomable universe there is a little planet where people laugh! I would therefore like to address this advice to all my human brothers and sisters:

DECIDE TO LAUGH,

Make others laugh,
Irradiate your good humour and happiness,
Coalesce with other happy people,
Look at the world with a wondrous smile,
Let the miracle of life well up in a happy face,
Grow and keep a twinkle in your eyes,
Laugh, sing, whistle and dance,
Wake up in the morning with a song in your heart,
Go to sleep with a happy thought on your mind.

Enliven any company with your cheerfulness,
Deflate tensions, depressions and bitterness
with good humour,
Be known as a happy, likeable, joyful person.

Tell jokes,
Read jokes,
Write down jokes,
Learn jokes by heart,
Look out for good humour everywhere,
For it is infinitely better for people
and nations
to laugh together
than to fight each other.

And at the hour of your death be able to say:
Life has been great fun,
thank you, O God,
for your beautiful, immensely
enjoyable gift.

HUMOUR AROUND THE PLANET

AFRICA

During World War II, Albert Schweitzer decided to stay in the African village of Lambarene. The Nazis tried to lure him back to Alsace-Lorraine. Goebbels wrote him a carefully composed letter which ended with the words "mit deutschem Gruss" (with German greetings) instead of the customary Heil Hitler. The great Alsatian doctor-philosopher wrote back, declining the Nazi offer, ending his letter with the words: "mit Afrikanischem Gruss" (with African greetings)!

*

When Schweitzer returned to Alsace-Lorraine after the war, a European friend asked him,

"You must be glad to be back in Europe. What do you think of civilization?"

Schweitzer answered: "It's a good idea. Let us start."

*

An African proverb often used at the UN when big power policies are discussed:

"When two elephants fight, it is the grass that gets hurt."

*

A French colonial landowner gave a bottle of wine to one of his African workers. A few days later he asked him if he liked it.

"It was just right."

"What do you mean?"

"Well, if it had been better you would not have given it to me, and if it had been worse I could not have drunk it. So, it was just right."

*

A French expert was leaving a government building in an African country when he saw a man sitting in the sun cleaning his nose in the old African way, closing one nostril and blowing the mucus onto the ground. The Frenchman made a disgusted face, took out a handkerchief, blew his nose in the western fashion and put the handkerchief back into his pocket.

The African who was watching him, commented wryly:

"You Westeners never throw anything away, do you!"

*

Former UN Secretary-General U Thant often said that spirituality had to catch up with materialism, science and technology. In order to illustrate his point, he used to tell the following story.

"One day a party of native bearers in Africa suddenly stopped, discharged their loads, sat down and refused to go forward. When asked for the reason, their leader said: Our bodies have gone too fast for our souls. We must wait for our souls to catch up with us."

*

A newly appointed American ambassador takes up his post in an African capital. Soon after his arrival, he instructs his aides to assemble the tribes in an open field, for he wants to talk to them. During his speech, the

Africans frequently interrupt him with a vast resounding chorus of "Bongo," "Bongo." The Ambassador is very pleased with himself, but as he walks back to his Cadillac, his Black driver points at something on the ground and says: "Mr. Ambassador, beware, do not step in the bongo!"

*

A technical assistance expert was hired to go to a very insalubrious African country. When discussing his contract with a UN personnel officer, he expressed surprise that no provision had been made for pension benefits. The UN official looked surprised and commented,

"My dear fellow, anyone going to that country need not worry about retirement!"

*

The President of a newly independent African country mentioned to a journalist,

"My government is deeply divided. Half of my ministers — including me — are pro-Russian; the other half — including me — are pro-American."

*

The president of the US was visiting the capital of a French-speaking African country. The leader of that country, wanting to welcome him in English, asked one of his colleagues to give him the English equivalent of "Je vous salue du fonds de mon coeur" (I greet you from the bottom of my heart).

When the US President arrived, the African President said,

"I greet you from the heart of my bottom." After a pause, he added proudly:

"And from my wife's, too!"

*

The wife of a western diplomat in Africa goes to the local market to buy vegetables. She finds reasonably fresh cauliflowers and asks the African woman who is selling them,

"Do they contain vitamins?"

African woman: "Well, there might be some. But don't worry. They will die when you cook them."

*

An African ambassador had brought a television set back to his country. One day, when he returned home from the office, he saw the set smashed up and asked what had happened. His aunt said:

"I was in front of that box with the children watching, when suddenly a big snake appeared and wanted to come out of it. To save the children, I destroyed the box."

*

In a UN meeting a diplomat from an African desert country says to two delegates from small countries who are fighting with each other:

"Beware of third powers. In my country we have a saying that when two men fight at a water hole, if they suddenly see vultures above them, they immediately stop fighting."

*

A comment on optimism and pessimism:

Two hat manufacturers sent salesmen to newly independent Africa.

A cable from the pessimistic salesman said: "Disastrous market. No one wears a hat in Africa. Am returning home."

Optimistic salesman: "Found a terrific market. No one is wearing a hat! Start producing immediately."

*

A World Health official was showing film projections with a greatly enlarged picture of the tset'se fly so as to explain to the villagers how the disease is transmitted. The health official asked,

"Are you now convinced that you must take action against this fly?" The head-man of the village answered,

"Oh no. We do not have such giant flies in our village!"

*

A South African Black arrives in heaven. He comments to St. Peter:

"I was in love with a white woman."

"When was that?" asks St. Peter.

"A half an hour ago."

*

An African diplomat was invited to an American dinner reception. When the food was passed around, the lady of the house asked him what kind of chicken meat he wanted. He answered: "The breast." The lady served him but remarked that one did not say "the breast" but "white meat."

The following day the African diplomat sent a corsage of flowers to the hostess with a little note thanking her and telling her that the corsage was to be affixed at her "white meat."

*

The elderly mother of an African UN official is traveling for the first time by airplane to New York. She complains to the stewardess that her ears hurt and is given chewing gum for relief. When the trip is over the stewardess asks the lady how she feels.

"Oh, I feel wonderful. It was a very thrilling experience and the chewing gum you gave me helped. But, could you please tell me how can I get it out of my ears?"

*

An African woman delegate to the UN does not know English very well. Sitting at a dinner party next to an American lady, she is asked,

"Do you have birth control in your country?" But the African woman had understood "Do you have bird control?" and answered

"Yes."

American lady: "What method do you use?"

"We limit the hunting season."

*

A psychiatrist was visiting an African diplomat at his home in New York and asked him,

"How do you feel? You were doing so well in the clinic that I felt you could stay at home from now on." The African replied, "Oh, I feel wonderful," as he walked around the room, spraying the walls with a repellent.

"What are you doing?" asks the doctor.

"I am spraying the walls to keep the elephants away."

"Elephants? They're thousands of miles away from here!"

With a broad, satisfied grin the african countered: "Well, you see, it works!"

*

A crocodile was sleeping with his wife. Several times during the night he woke up during nightmares, shouting:

"Down with capitalism!"

"Hail Fidel Castro!"

"Down with the CIA and the Pentagon!"

The following morning his wife said to him: "How many times do I have to tell you not to eat a Communist before bedtime!"

*

An African student's answer to the question:

"What is a gubernatorial race?"

"The white race."

"Why?"

"Because they always want to govern and boss around the whole world."

*

There is an African tribe which does not eat eggs nor drink milk. They give their children Carnation milk, however, because they believe it comes from flowers.

*

When the cannibals saw the first American baby food jars with pictures of little babies they called them "ground babies."

*

There was a UN chaplain the cannibals could not boil. He was a friar.

*

Two cannibal chiefs talking to each other:
"I just don't like my mother-in-law."
"Well, then, just eat the vegetables."

*

An African family of diplomats once placed this ad in the Diplomatic World Bulletin:
"We are looking for a vegetarian baby-sitter."

*

An African delegate to the UN was voting in the strangest way. After having voted well on one issue, to the dismay of his African colleagues, he voted in favour of South Africa the next issue. They came running to him, chattering furiously: "What got into you? Why did you vote against the interests of your African brethren?" "Well, the only instructions I have from my government is to vote in a well-balanced way. In order to do so, I vote once in favour, and then I vote against; the third time I abstain."

*

The wife of an African UN diplomat went to the Bronx zoo with her children, wanting to see the giraffe. The zoo attendant informed her that they were late — the zoo was closed.

"I am here with my twelve children. They will be so disappointed."

"Twelve children, you said, lady?"

"Yes."

"Well, in that case I am going to let the giraffe out. She has got to see that.!"

*

A New York dentist asked a UN African client,

"Could you pay for a dental plate if I found one necessary?"

And the shrewd African replied:

"Would you find one necessary if I couldn't pay for it?"

*

Three officers from UN forces, a Frenchman, an Englishman and a Russian were captured by cannibals. The chief of the tribe inquired about their last wishes.

Frenchman: "I would like to smoke a Gauloise."

Englishman: "I would like to write a letter to my wife."

Russian: "I would like you to kick me in the behind."

The chief responds and the Russian draws a gun from his shirt and kills the chief and the surrounding cannibals.

His two friends ask, utterly shocked:

"Why did you wait so long, Ivan? We didn't know that you had a gun hidden."

Ivan: "I could shoot only after there had been a clear case of aggression."

*

Assistant to the Secretary-General of the UN:

"Sir, here is a cable from Africa. Chief X thanks you

for the 200 UN soldiers you sent him."

Secretary-General: "Does he comment on them?"

"Yes, he says that they were delicious!"

*

A cannibal travels for the first time by plane to New York to attend a UN meeting. The air hostess shows him the menu. After examining it he asks her:

"Could you rather show me the passenger list."

*

The chief of the cannibal tribe asks his UN prisoner:

"What is your profession?"

"I am a UN newspaper man."

"A chief editor?"

"No, only an assistant editor."

"Well, cheer up, you are going to have a promotion! Soon you will be editor in chief!"

*

A cannibal was putting a bag of dried powder into a cup of hot water. A UNer asked him what it was:

Cannibal: "Instant man."

*

UNer in Africa: "Why do you look so intently at me?"

Cannibal: "I am the food inspector."

*

During the Congo crisis, a group of Tunisian financial advisers were hired by the UN to take over functions formerly handled by the Belgians. A Congolese asked them,

"How long have you been independent?"

"Five years."

"And you are already all white!"

*

UN official to cannibal:

"You were educated in Europe and yet you still eat human flesh?"

Cannibal: "Yes, but I eat it with a fork!"

*

Two Africans meet a priest in the jungle. He wears his arm in a sling. They ask him what has happened to him.

"I fell in my bathtub and broke my arm."

After the priest has left, the first African asks the second:

"What is a bathtub?"

"I don't know. I am not a Catholic."

*

A Bishop visited a missionary church deep in the jungles of Africa. On Sunday morning he was shocked to see the entire flock of villagers attend mass nude.

"Couldn't you ask them to dress for mass?" he asked the priest.

"I did. But all they did was giggle at each other's clothes, so I had to ask them to come to church naked again."

*

A UN official on his birthday was working late in his Congo office. His secretary invited him for a cocktail at her apartment. When they arrived, she served him a cocktail and withdrew to the bedroom.

The official enjoyed his drink while undressing, waiting for her return. After a while the bedroom door opened and she called: "Please come in."

The UN official walked in, nude, as the lights went on, and the singing: "Happy birthday to you!" by all his office colleagues.

*

A UN soldier got lost in the African jungle. After days of tortuous hiking, he finally reached a village at the entrance of which he saw a dead man hanging from a gibbet.

"Thank God! I am back in civilization!" he exclaimed.

*

During the Congo crisis, there was such a mess in the country that a native once asked a UN official:

"When will independence at long last end?"

*

When the African countries became independent, a French-speaking African delegate complained on behalf of Africa in a speech at the UN Economic Commission,

"We Africans of the francophone group do firmly protest against the preferential treatment given to the saxophones in the United Nations."

*

A newly appointed Congolese staff member, arriving at the UN in New York, paid a visit to the personnel office where a young French-speaking lady took good care of him.

"Etes-vous Belge, Mademoiselle?" ("Are you Belgian, Miss?")

"Non, je suis Francaise." ("No, I am French.")

"Eh! Bien, je vous felicite. Pour une Francaise, vous parlez rudement bien le Belge!" ("Well, I congratulate you. For a French girl, you speak Belgian remarkably well!")

*

US lady to an African diplomat:

"Do you like parrots?"

"Yes, I love them cooked in peanut-oil."

*

In former French colonies and overseas territories, people used to name their children after the saint's name appearing on the French calendar on the day of birth. As a result, many Africans today have such Christian names as Armistice and Fete Nat. (National Holiday)!

*

Two UN soldiers were patrolling the jungle in the Congo. Suddenly a lion leaped out of the bushes, grabbing one of the men and begins to drag him off.

"Shoot!" yells the victim to his friend.

"I can't," answers the other, "I've run out of film."

*

A UN chaplain, meeting a lion in the jungle, kneels down, closes his eyes and prays to the Almighty,

"Dear God, please transform this beast into a devout Christian."

After a while, he opens his eyes and he sees the lion kneeling down and praying:

"Dear God, may you bless the meal which I am about to take."

*

A hungry lion met Dag Hammarksjold in the jungle but did not touch him. Another lion asked him what was wrong.

"He is half grit and half backbone."

*

A Dominican and a Jesuit were sent as missionaries to an African country. The Dominican challenged the Jesuit:

"Let us see who converts the largest number of aborigenes."

After a year the two met again.
Dominican: "I converted 345 heathens."
Jesuit: "I did better: I converted the king."

*

In an African village a missionary is called to a hut where a young African lies feverish. After giving him an injection of penicillin he says,

"Young man, no need worry. You soon ok and work again like elephant."

Young African: "You very good. When me ok, me return to Paris to resume my lecturing at Sorbonne on nuclear physics."

ASIA

AUSTRALIA

A UN official who had a car accident in Australia was taken unconscious to a hospital for surgery. The following morning he asked the Australian nurse,

"Was I brought here to die?"

Nurse: "No. You were brought in yesterdie."

*

On a guided tour of the Bronx Zoo in New York, a group arrived at the kangaroo cage where the guide told them:

"This is a native of Australia."

A woman almost fainted and exclaimed:

"Oh, my God, my sister married one!"

*

Father kanguru:

"And where is the baby?"

Mother kanguru:

"Good God, someone has stolen my pouch!"

*

An Australian was trying, but failing to impress a visiting Texan with the wonders of Australia. Then a kangaroo hopped past them.

"Well, I grant you one thing," the Texan said. "Your grasshoppers are bigger than ours."

*

CHINA

The Soviet Union and China are at war. During the first week the Russians take one million prisoners, the second week five million and at the end of the month, they have thirty million Chinese prisoners. At that point, the Russian leaders receive the following cable from Peking:

"We hope that by now you have understood the situation. Are you ready to capitulate?"

*

A war between the Soviet Union and China has ended. The president of China has invited the president of the United States to visit what is left of the Soviet Union.

The US president asks: "How shall we be travelling?" and the Chinese president responds: "By bicycle."

"And what shall we do in the afternoon?"

*

A Chinese official travels for the first time to America. In New York City he takes a subway and writes back to his friends,

"This country is still very backward. Thirty years after the war they still have to buy tokens to take the subway."

*

Shortly after President Nixon's visit to China, an American doctor followed as part of a cultural exchange. While visiting the hospital, the doctor sat next to a patient lying under an oxygen tent to talk to him, but the sick man knew no English. The patient became very restless, his face turned red and blue, he seized his temperature chart, scribbled some Chinese on it, showed it to the American doctor and died! The American, deeply shocked, cannot understand what has happened; can hardly believe that the mere sight of an American could kill a Chinese! A Chinese doctor entered and seized the temperature chart clasped in the hand of the deceased. The dying man had written, "You are sitting on my oxygen line!"

*

A Jew says to a Chinese:

"We are about ten million people. How many are you?"

Chinese: "Over a billion."

Jew: "How come that one hears so little about you?"

Chinese: "Well, when you are as many as we are you don't have to make so much noise."

*

A childless couple adopted a Chinese baby and so decide to take Chinese lessons. The teacher ask them what induced them to learn that language.

"In about a year our adopted child will start to talk and we want to be able to understand him."

*

A widower was arranging flowers on his deceased wife's tomb when he saw a Chinaman place a bowl of rice on the tomb next to it. Smiling he asked:

"Are you foolish enough to believe that she will come out and eat your rice?"

And the Chinaman replied: "She is as likely to do that as your wife is to come and smell your flowers."

*

Shortly after the creation of the UN, a reception was given by a rich American lady in her apartment at the Waldorf Astoria. When Victor Hoo, the Chinese Under Secretary-General rang the bell and the lady opened the door, she exclaimed:

"Oh, you must be the laundryman!"

To this, Victor Hoo answered gently:

"Madam, it is quite possible that all laundrymen in this country are Chinese, but it does not necessarily follow that all Chinese are laundrymen."

*

A UN official asked a young Chinese staff member recently recruited from China:

"What is the matter with you? Why is your face all bandaged around the mouth?"

"I am learning how to eat with a fork."

*

A Chinese woman visited a United States gynecologist for the first time.

"I have been married for twelve years and have not been able to have a baby."

Doctor: "We will see to that. Please lie down on this table."

Bewildered Chinese lady: "But I would have preferred that it be a Chinese baby."

*

Mao Tse Tung once said,

"Our forefathers were wise people. They invented printing but avoided publishing newspapers. They invented gunpowder but never made arms. They invented the compass but were careful not to discover America."

*

War communique in the year 2000:

"All is quiet on the Chinese-Finnish front."

*

During his visit to China, Nixon asked Mao Tse Tung,

"Do you think the world would be the same today if Khrushchev instead of Kennedy had been assassinated?"

"I wouldn't know, but I do know that Aristotle Onassis would never have married Mrs. Khrushchev!"

*

Chinese to American:

"We make it a point to settle all our debts on New Year's Day."

American: "You are lucky your New Year is not preceded by Christmas."

*

A psychiatrist asks a woman patient:

"What is your name?"

"Mrs. Mao Tse Tung."

"But, last time you told me that you were Mrs. John Kennedy."

"Yes, but I got remarried."

*

A Chinese pupil is being asked by his teacher,

"Who is your father?"

"Mao Tse Tung."

"And who is your mother?"

"The cultural revolution."

"And what do you want to become?"

"An orphan!"

*

A Chinese leader commented that,

"The Russian leaders say that they will win a war against us, but an increasing number of Russian people are learning how to eat caviar with chopsticks!"

★

When Italy's Premier Aldo Moro visited the People's Republic of China, he insisted on attending mass in Peking on Sunday morning. The Chinese agreed and opened for service an old dilapidated church. The diplomatic community in Peking was amazed that the Italian Premier had achieved such a success and they decided to petition the Chinese government asking that the church remain open on Sundays for the Catholic diplomatic community. Thus, the Chinese circulated a questionnaire asking how many people would attend mass, and every Catholic from the diplomatic missions signed up. As a result, they were informed that the church would remain open. A few days later another circular was distributed announcing that on the following Sunday the famous Emperor's tombs in the North of China would be open to diplomatic visitors for the first time ever. Most diplomats could not resist and signed up for the visit of the tombs. And a few days later, the Chinese closed the Catholic church again, saying that since nobody attended the service, there was no point in keeping it open!

★

Mao Tse Tung asked his preferred sculptor for a conference.

"I want you to make a huge statue of Karl Marx."

"Very good," said the sculptor. "And what subject do you envisage?"

"You will show him discovering true socialism by reading my Little Red Book."

★

A Chinese student who had been invited to his first dinner with a US family prepared for the occasion by memorizing phrases from an etiquette book. When his host passed him food, the young man responded, "Thank you, Sir or Madam, as the case may be."

★

A UN employee sent a letter from China. At the end of it, he wrote, "I hope this letter will pass the Chinese censorship."

The letter arrived with a note in it.

"There is no censorship in the People's Republic of China."

*

When Victor Hoo was Chinese Under Secretary-General at the UN, his friend Yu was Ambassador of China in Washington and this was the origin of endless jokes concerning telephone conversations between the two. For example, Yu, calling Hoo, asks, "Is this you?"

"No, I am Hoo and who are you?"

"I am Yu."

Or... "Is this Yu?"

"No, I am Hoo. You have the wong number." etc., etc.

*

A Chinese proverb often quoted at the UN:

"Before you can walk in another person's shoes, you must take off your own shoes."

*

Shortly after the People's Republic of China admission of to the UN, a UN lady official was invited to visit China. She was shown many fascinating sights and was asked every day if there was something else she wanted to see. She answered: "Yes, before leaving China I would like to meet Premier Chou En Lai." The Chinese guide, for her part, asked her each time if she would like to see the Chinese revolutionary ballets, but she expressed no interest. Then during the last week, the Chinese guide one morning announced to her:

"Premier Chou En Lai will be happy to meet you tomorrow evening during the performance of the Chinese revolutionary ballets at the Peking Opera!"

*

When President Nixon visited China, Mao Tse Tung told him that the Chinese had discovered America long before the Vikings, Christopher Columbus and Amerigo Vespucci. Nixon expressed surprise.

"But there is no record of it, no trace whatsoever." And Mao Tse Tung said, "Well, our discoverers looked around and when they saw that your inhabitants were living naked, they concluded there was no point in staying: no business for Chinese laundrymen."

*

A Chinese teacher was explaining to children the difference between hell and paradise.

"In hell you will see people sitting around an enormous heap of delicious fried rice, but they cannot eat it because attached to the end of their hands are chopsticks which are so long that they cannot bring the food to their mouths. As a result, they are starving. In paradise you will also see people sitting around a heap of fried rice, and they, too, have long chopsticks attached at their hands, but they are well-fed and happy because they feed each other."

*

Mao Tse Tung once sent the following telegram to Khrushchev: THERE IS TERRIBLE HUNGER IN CHINA STOP PLEASE SEND FOODSTUFFS STOP

Kruschev answered: TIGHTEN YOUR BELTS STOP

Whereupon Mao Tse Tung cabled back: PLEASE SEND BELTS STOP

*

The President of Greece went to visit China to discuss with Mao Tse Tung problems between the two countries. During the meeting the President of China asked: "How many Greeks are you? (meaning how many people were in his party)"

"We are 9 million people."

"And in what hotel are you staying?"

*

*

To predict the future of China is about as difficult as it was to forecast what Sophia Loren would look like from her picture when she made her first communion.

*

A world weather report in the year 2000:

"Both over the North and the South poles the sky is clouded. For the rest of China, the weather is fair."

*

In the early 1900s, when Germany sent troops to China, several Alsatians were shipped to Shanghai. On the first day of their arrival, a German officer overheard two of them speak together. One said:

"Chang, son shin shen hiet." The second one answered:

"Yo, Hon, son ish shen."

German officer: "You Alsatians are fantastic! You are here only one day, and already you speak Chinese!"

(In Alsatian dialect, what they said was: "John, the sun shines beautifully today. "Yes, Johannes, the sun is gorgeous."

*

INDIA

Prior to India's independence, an American journalist once asked a Hindu journalist:

"If England were to leave India, wouldn't you be afraid that anarchy would erupt all over your country."

"Yes, probably."

"And that the local princes and maharajaj would reestablish their tyranny?"

"Yes, I suppose so."

"Why then do you want to become independent?"

"Because it will be *our* anarchy and *our* tyranny!"

*

A missionary tried to convert a Hindu to Catholicism, but the Hindu obstinately refuses. However, the priest persisted:

"Don't you want to go to heaven?"

"No, because I don't believe in heaven."

"Why?"

"Because if there were such a place, the British would have grabbed it a long time ago."

*

A young Sikh official of the UN is sitting in a bus in New York City when an elderly lady boards the vehicle. He offers her politely his seat. At the end of the journey, when the old lady gets off the bus, she turns to the turbaned man:

"Thank you, young man; I hope your headache will get better."

*

A Sikh commenting to another Sikh in the streets of New Delhi:

"Did you see how weak the sun shines today? It is hard to believe that it is giving us daylight."

Second Sikh: "You are mistaken. What you see is not the sun but the moon."

A quarrel ensues. Another Sikh passes by and is asked for his opinion.

He looks up at the sky and says:

"I really could not tell. I am not from New Delhi and I am therefore not familiar with this part of the country."

*

An Indian teacher asked his class,

"How do you stop a herd of elephants from charging?"

"By taking away their credit cards!"

*

Indian optimist:
"I would like to do something great and clean."
"Why don't you wash an elephant?"

*

Movies were being shown for the first time in a remote Indian village and an old man returned again and again, not missing a single performance. Someone asked him,

"Why do you keep on seeing the same movie?"

"Well, there is a scene where a young girl is undressing. A train passes in front of her just before she finishes. But some day that train is bound to be late!"

*

An American diplomat is driving on an Indian country road at a very high speed. Suddenly an Indian bullock cart comes out of a field and blocks the road. The American diverts his car from the road into the field from which the cart had just come. The car turns over, explodes and the driver is killed.

One of the Indian peasants who was leading the bullock cart says to his companion,

"By the Lord Shiva, how lucky we are! Did you see? We just came out of that field in time!"

*

A journalist asks the President of India,

"What do you do for law and order in the country?"

"For law I turn to the Minister of Justice and for order I turn to Mrs. Gandhi."

*

When the French establishment of Goa in India was seized by the Indian military, the Indian Minister of Defense, Krishna Menon, was nicknamed at the UN "Goa constrictor."

*

The son of an Indian UN staff member wrote this in an essay at the UN International School after having had an operation:

"A nurse came near my bed, stuck a needle in me and I disappeared!"

*

An Indian and an American, talking about insomnia, said,

"I suffer terribly from insomnia. The other night I counted up to 3652 trees until I could sleep."

And the American replied: "Why don't you count sheep like everyone else?"

"Oh, no, I couldn't. I am a vegetarian!"

*

An Indian male, visiting a population-control center in his country, asked for a vasectomy. The doctor congratulated him for his wise decision and asked how he had arrived at it.

"Did you read any literature issued by the UN Fund for Population Activities or hear of the decisions of the World Population Conference?"

"No."

"Did your wife request it? Had she heard of the recommendations of the UN World Conference on Women?"

"No, it was a decision of the children."

"Oh, yes?"

"Yes, my wife and I decided to put it to the vote of the children; They favoured it 14 to 1."

*

JAPAN

An American businessman arriving at a Tokyo hotel, engaged a Japanese bell-hop. The American is eager to learn some Japanese and he asks the boy:

"How do you say goodbye?"

"Sayonara."

"And how do you say good morning?"

"Ohio." The following morning when a waiter brings the American his breakfast, he tries to remember the word the boy had taught him, but he cannot. Suddenly his face lights up and he says:

"Oklahoma!"

*

Before WW II American goods were considered highly superior to Japanese goods. In order to expand the sales of their products abroad, several Japanese firms established their headquarters in a little town called USA, so that they could send out their merchandise marked "Made in USA."

*

There is the story of the Japanese diplomat who, when speaking to the UN General Assembly's economic and financial committee, referred to the "flea market" instead of the "free market."

*

An elderly Alsatian who had inherited a substantial fortune wondered what he would do with all the money. Since he had never left his native village of Bergheim he thought he would take a faraway trip. Having read in the newspapers that Olympic Games were being held in

Saporo, Japan, he decided to go there. He went to the railroad station and asked a ticket for Saporo. The stationmaster looked at him with utter surprise:

"Are you crazy? All I can do is give you a train ticket to Strasbourg. From there on you will have to see how you can get to Saporo."

In Strasbourg the same thing happened. All they did was to give him a railroad ticket to Paris. In Paris too they refused to give him an airticket to Saporo and gave him one only to Tokyo wherefrom he had to take a Japanese line to Saporo.

He attended the games happily and towards the end suddenly remembered that he had no return ticket and reservations. He went to the Saporo office of Japan Airlines where he was received by a Japanese hostess. "Could I have a ticket to Bergheim in Alsace?"

Hostess: "Certainly, Sir. Do you want Oberbergheim or Unterbergheim?"

*

Japanese Minister Taniguchi, a delegate to the United Nations, once called the Toyota's New York Office about buying a car. To the girl who answered the telephone he said,

"This is Taniguchi, Minister from the Japanese mission."

The girl interrupted, "I am sorry, but we do not give to religious groups."

*

A Japanese beggar went to see God to complain about his misery.

"You must take a long-term view. For example, up here a million years are only a second."

"And what is worth a million yen?"

"Only a cent."

"Could you then give me a cent."

"Yes, wait a second."

*

Japan was accused at the UN of overfishing — depleting the seas' and oceans' living resources.
A delegate asked the Japanese ambassador,
"What do you do with all that fish you catch?"
"We eat what we can."
"And what do you do with the rest?"
"We can what we can't eat."

*

When you go to a Japanese bath nude in Hokkaido or Kyushu, you can see very little because of the heavy steam. However, there are a few inches above the water's surface where one can see clearly. All you see is other eyes!

*

"I just bought an American television."
Wife: "Do you understand American?"

*

THAILAND

Definition of a UN or foreign expert by the Prime Minister of Thailand:
"A foreign expert is someone who comes in to find out and get out before we find out."

*

In a speech to the United Nations Economic and Social Commission for Asia and the Pacific in Bangkok, the Thai delegate launched a violent attack against the USSR. The delegates, listening to his long, fiery diatribe, suddenly hear him accuse the Soviet Union for spreading its testicles all over Asia! He had meant to say tentacles!

*

What prevented the Vietnamese from invading the whole of Thailand?

The Bangkok traffic jam!

LATIN AMERICA

A Latin American dictator accompanied to the airport the president of the United States who has just paid an official visit.

"Adios, Aguila del Norte" (Goodbye, Eagle of the North).

The President of the United States reciprocates with: "Adios, Ojo de Pato" (Goodbye, Eye of a Duck).

On the way back to the capital, the dictator asks his aide,

"What strange greetings they use in America! Why did he call me Eye of a Duck?"

The embarrassed aide replies,

"I am afraid to tell you the truth."

"I insist. Otherwise I will have you shot!"

"Well, if you insist. The U.S. president's Spanish is less than perfect! What he really meant to say was,

"Adios, Hijo de Puta (Goodbye, son of a bitch!")."

*

Someone remarked to Theodore Roosevelt that such and such a dictator in Latin America was a son-of-a-bitch.

Roosevelt replied with a satisfied grin,

"Yes, but he is "*our* son-of-a-bitch."

*

A man imprisoned within in a Latin American dictatorship is asked how long is his sentence.

"Twenty years."

"What did you do?"

"Nothing."

"That cannot be."

"Why?"

"Because for nothing you get only ten years."

*

In a Latin American dictatorship the chief of the secret police goes to a remote barbershop in the capital city and asks the barber,

"Do you know who I am?"

"No."

"Ok, in that case you can give me a shave."

*

In a Latin American dictatorship where there is a lot of guerrilla activity, a priest one Sunday goes up to the pulpit and admonishes the congregation:

"I have had it. Every day you come to confess murders of generals, machinegunning of government forces, and the blowing up of highways and bridges. I must remind you that I want to hear sins, not political acts."

*

A Latin American general-dictator was known for his love of medals and decorations and displayed them all over his chest. One day during a reception in his residence, the dictator's butler fell down the stairs, dropping a large tray of cutlery.

His wife came running, thinking that it was her husband!

"Did you hurt yourself, darling?"

*

An American expert proposed for a Latin American country the construction of a road to link distant hill villages with the capital and asks one of the villagers,

"How long does it take you to transport your products by mule from the village to the capital?"

"Three days."

"Well, you see, with a good road it will take you only one day."

"And what will we do with the other two days?"

*

A Latino, arriving for the first time in New York, thirsty, sees a soft-drink vending machine, inserts a quarter and a sign lights up, "No sale."

The Latino does not believe his eyes

"Those Gringos are fantastic! How did their machine guess that I speak Spanish?"

(In Spanish *No sale* means "it does not come out".)

*

An American businessman staying at a hotel in a Latin American country goes to the lobby and asks a freckled brunette working in the cashier's office,

"Could you have dinner with me tonight?"

She is surprised, but accepts the invitation.

During the dinner she asks,

"Why did you ever think that I would accept?"

"It was all written in the Bible."

Later he asks her whether he can accompany her to her apartment.

She accepts again and when they are intimate with each other asks how he had guessed that she would allow intimacy.

"Oh, as I said, it was all written in the Bible."

Returning to his hotelroom, he took from the night table the Bible placed in each room. On the first page, someone had written,

"The girl with the freckles in the cashier's office is easy to sleep with," and wrote under it,

"That is correct."

*

The foreman of a construction team in New York City chides a newly arrived Latino,

"Why are you carrying only four bricks when the other men are carrying eight?"

"Well, I'm not too lazy to make two trips!"

*

Jose, a newly immigrated Puerto Rican to the US, tells his friend Pedro that he received a magnificent reception at the Yankee Stadium.

"They let me climb on the flagpole and then they all sang, "JOSE CAN YOU SEE"!"

*

The three greatest dangers in Latin America are Chilean women, Peruvian friends and Bolivian politicians.

*

When the American car Nova was sold in Latin America, the producers were astonished that the car did not sell at all, until someone told them that *no va* in Spanish means it does not run!

*

Costa Rica is so much in debt that it receives a million dollars in aid every day from the United States. The Nicaraguans call them "Costa-Reagans."

*

BRAZIL

Two Brazilian workers take the same bus every day from the suburbs to Rio de Janeiro. One of them had enrolled in an evening adult course and every morning he was asking some historical questions to his friend:

"Do you know who Pedro Alvarez Cabral was?"

"No".

"Well, he was the Portugese navigator who discovered Brazil."

Another day he asked him:

"Do you know who Diego Alvarez Correa was?"

"No."

"Well, he was the real founder of Brazil. He established the first permanent settlement in our country."

And it went on like that for days, until one morning the second worker could not hold it any longer, and he said to his friend:

"May I also ask you a question?"

"Yes, of course."

"Do you know who Santos is?"

"You mean, Santos Dumont, our famous aviator?"

"No, I mean Joao Santos."

"Joao Santos?"

"Well, he is the guy who every evening makes love to your wife while you are taking the adults' course!"

*

The Brazilian internal revenue system was trying to track down some notorious tax evadors. Among them was a flashy young man who had a tremendous standard of living but no visible source of income. They questioned him and asked where he derived his money from.

"I am betting and I win all my bets."

Tax official: "Let us see."

Young man: "OK. I bet I can extract a tooth of mine with my fingers."

The tax official bets that he cannot and the young man takes out of his mouth with his fingers an artificial tooth.

The superior of the tax official also wants to bet.

Young man: "I bet that I can remove one of my eyes from its socket."

And indeed he wins again by taking out a glass eye from its socket.

The head of the tax office comes in at that point and he wants to bet too.

Young man: "I bet you have a big scar on the left side of your belly."

Tax man: "I take this bet immediately."

They withdraw to a more intimate room and the tax official undresses to show that indeed he has no scar.

The young man comments philosophically: "You are right. I lose this bet, but I am winning a much bigger one from one of your colleagues with whom I bet that I would be able to have you undress in front of me."

*

CHILE

Don Pedro, don Sanchez and don Otto meet every evening at the pub. Don Otto seldom talks, but to whatever his friends say, he always responds with,

"It could be worse."

One evening, don Pedro reported that one of their friends had come home unexpectedly and found his wife with another man. He killed the woman, the lover and himself.

"It could be worse," don Otto commented as usual.

"How could it be worse?" exclaimed don Pedro.

"I said that he killed his wife, the lover and himself!"

"It could have been worse. If he had returned the day before he would have killed me!"

*

It is said that the only virgin in Chile is the Virgin of the Cerro San Cristobal because she is in concrete and thirty feet tall.

*

Don Otto and don Pedro meet at a bar. Don Pedro says to don Otto:

"I hate doing this to you, but I must tell you that when I passed by your home, the curtains of the bedroom were open and I saw your wife making love with a fellow."

"Did you recognize him?"

"No."

"Was he a short, stocky fellow?"

"Yes."

"Did he have hairy legs?"

"Yes."

"Was he bald?"

"Yes."

"Well, then it is don Arturo. He is not very choosy. He makes love with any woman."

*

Don Pedro to don Otto:

"You know, passing by your house, through the window I saw your wife making love with a friend."

Don Otto went home and later when he saw don Pedro answered.

"You were mistaken. He was not a friend."

*

(During the Allende regime)

A Chilean "roto" is being politically indoctrinated. An Allende man asks him:

"Don Pedro, if you had a villa in Vina del Mar, wouldn't you share it with one of your friends from the working class?"

"Yes, Senor, I would."

"And if you had a Cadillac, wouldn't you share it too with your comrades?"

"Yes, Senor, I would."

"And wouldn't you share your chickens with your friends?"

"Under no circumstance would I."

"Why not?"

"Because I happen to have chickens."

*

Two communist workers were patrolling a rich neighbourhood in Santiago. They arrived at a place where garbage cans were being kept. There they saw a woman half immersed in one of the cans. They went near her and discovered that she did not move. It was a maid who had fainted over her job. One of the workers inspected her and commented sadly to his friend:

"Can you imagine how wasteful those capitalists are. This woman is still perfectly usable, and they threw her away!"

*

Some of the Chilean ministers appointed by Allende were poorly educated and hence the object of many jokes. For example,it was told that one of them after leaving a cabinet meeting ordered an assistant to bring some round paper sheets.

"Why round paper?"

"Because President Allende asked me to issue a circular."

*

A minister, visiting the United States and very thirsty, found a soft-drink vending machine. He approached it and saw written on it: "Dime," whereupon he bent close to the machine and whispered, "Quiero uno Coca Cola." "*Dime,*" in Spanish means Tell me, and so he answered: I would like a Coca Cola.

*

The Minister of Interior reporting to General Pinochet:

"Robbers have penetrated last night into the Ministry."

"Have they stolen anything?"

"Yes. The results of the next elections!"

*

A Chilean was swimming in a sea infested by sharks. When he returned to the seashore, his friends were surprised that nothing had happened to him.

"Oh, they did not bother me at all. I have a tattoo on my chest saying that President Pinochet is the greatest Chilean president ever. Not a single shark would swallow that."

*

(Chilean jokes during the Pinochet regime)

A Chilean official had a picture of Chile's national hero — Bernardo O'Higgins — hanging in his office. One day, to his utter astonishment he saw O'Higgins' lips move.

"Bring me a horse. I have to put order in this country."

The frightened official ran to get his minister who was an army general. The general looked at the picture and O'Higgins chided,

"I told you to bring me a horse, not an ass."

*

CUBA

Do you know how Che Guevara became Minister of Economy in Cuba?

After his victory over Batista, Castro assembled his friends and asked them: "Is there an economist among you?"

Che Guevara raised his hand and he was made Minister of Economy.

After a few months, Castro became dubious of Guevara'a capacities as an economist. He asked him:

"Where did you study economics?"

"I never studied economics."

"Why then did you raise your hand?"

"I thought you had asked who is a communist."

*

Cuba is the greatest country in the world: it has its capital in Moscow, its soldiers in Africa and its population in the United States.

*

PERU

In a Peruvian village a donkey kicked to death a peasant's mother-in-law. When she was buried, the whole male population of the village flocked to the church. After the funeral, the priest expressed his joy to the peasant:

"Your mother-in-law was liked very much. I have never seen so many people in my church."

Peasant: "They didn't come for the funeral. They came to buy the donkey!"

MIDDLE EAST

When the Arabs resorted to the oil squeeze against Western countries supporting Israel, Premier Golda Meir threw her hands up and addressed the Almighty in these terms.

"O God, why did you lead your chosen people to the only place in the Middle East where there is no oil?"

*

An Israeli teacher asked his class in Tel Aviv:

"Who was Moses?"

Little boy: "An idiot."

Teacher: "Why do you say that?"

"If after having crossed the Red Sea he had turned to the right instead of the left, we would have all that oil today!"

*

The elders of a village in the Middle East were discussing the new coming of the Messiah. They decided to post an old man at the entrance of the village to watch out for Him. The old man sat there for one month, two months, three months and finally went back to the elders complaining:

"I have been sitting there for three months without seeing any Messiah. By the way, you are paying me much too little for that job. I want a raise."

The elders deliberated and gave him their answer:

"We are not going to give you a raise. You should be satisfied, you have a good, steady job."

*

During a meeting between President Nixon and Mrs. Golda Meier, the President of the United States said,

"Mrs. Meier, let us try once and for all to settle the Middle East conflict, because we have a unique opportunity: both our ministers of foreign affairs are Jewish — Abba Eban and Kissinger."

"Yes, Mr. President, but there is a big difference between the two; ours speaks good English."

*

When Moses came down from Mount Sinai he said to his people,

"I have both good news and bad news for you. The good news is that God's commandments have been reduced to ten. The bad news is that adultery is still in."

*

God meets with Jesus, Moses, and Muhammed and suggests that they return to Earth and try to settle the Middle East problem.

Jesus: "I decline, because the first time I went down there they crucified me."

Moses: "I did my duty bringing the Israelis from Egypt through the Red Sea. I consider this is quite enough."

*

Secretary of State Kissinger was given some choice cloth by his hosts during a visit to China. On his stop-over in Hong-Kong he visited a tailor to order a suit and was told there was not enough cloth for a suit. Kissinger then tried tailors in London and in Rome who told him exactly the same thing. When he arrived in Israel, he went to see a Jewish tailor who examined the material and said,

"How many suits do you want, one or two?"

Kissinger was surprised and related his experiences with the tailors from Hong Kong, London and Rome. How could he make two suits with the same material?

"Well, Mr. Secretary of State, after all you are not such a big man!"

*

The Israeli cabinet met in secret session with the prime minister reporting that the situation was serious: the prolonged Middle East conflict is weakening the country. Inflation is rampant. The people are discouraged. The future is very gloomy. He asks for proposals.

One cabinet member suggests that Israel declare war against the United States.

"Then, after the defeat, they will do with us what they did with Germany and Japan: they will help us become a great, prosperous nation."

But the Prime Minister remains somber and says,

"Yes, but suppose we win?"

*

An Israeli was working in a baby-carriages factory stealing every day a part in order to have a free baby-carriage for his expectant wife.

When he had them all, he worked for hours trying to assemble them, but finally he gave up and said to his wife,

"Darling, I have tried every possible combination, but each produces a machine gun."

*

Muhammed: "What is the use? Look at these multitudes of fanatic Moslems. Do you think my teachings have had any effects? No, there is no point in trying again."

Then, they suddenly have an idea and they suggest that God might go down to Earth himself.

"Under no circumstance", said God. "The first thing you would do is to start a Middle-East conflict up here!"

*

The leader of an Eastern socialist country visits Israel. Upon arrival he is given a beautiful suite in the best hotel in Tel Aviv. After he has settled down, he wants to talk to his advisers, but they have all disappeared. He enquires from the hotel desk where they may have gone and is told that they all went to visit their relatives!

*

After an appalling number of accidents in the military zones of Israel, General Yadin decided to introduce drastic speed limits and penalties which were enforced with utmost severity. One day a fast-moving car, sighted by the military police, is chased and stopped. The reckless driver happens to be General Dayan; but he expresses shock.

"General Yadin's rules are meant for drivers who have two eyes. How could you expect me to keep my only eye on the road *and* on the speedometer?"

*

During the troubles in Lebanon, a guy who was looting a store saw another man putting goods from that same store into a car and said clumsily,

"You have been taking much more stuff than I!"

"Well, there is good reason; I am the store's owner."

*

What are the three shortest texts on Earth:
- the Jewish code of ethics
- the list of victorious Arab generals
- Who is who in Albania

*

A Jew boards a plane and finds only one seat vacant between two Arabs. To avoid any trouble, he takes his shoes off, places a newspaper on his face and pretends to go to sleep. After a while the Arab on his left asks him to fetch him a cup of coffee. To avoid trouble, the Jew abides and when he returns with the coffee he sees human excrement in one of his shoes. He does not say anything and pretends to go back to sleep. After a while the second Arab asks him to fetch a cup of coffee. On his return, the Jew finds excrement in his second shoe. The Arabs then engage in a conversation with him.

"Tell us, Jew, what do you think of the international situation?"

"Oh! It is fine. Detente between the US and the USSR is making good progress and there is no longer any danger of a world war."

"And what do you think of the Middle East situation?"

"Oh! There, unfortunately, I do not see any hope as long as Arabs defecates into a Jew's shoes and as long as a Jew urinates into their coffee."

*

A story heard at the UN committee for the standardization of citrus fruits goes as follows:

A New York Jew decided to settle down permanently in Israel. When he arrived in Tel Aviv his best friend was waiting for him at the airport and asked him why on Earth he had decided to emigrate from the United States.

He answered: "Because of the intolerable discrimination against the Jews."

"What? You must be kidding! We hold practically all power in New York. It is rather the other way around."

*

"Not at all. I am telling you the truth. It has become frankly intolerable. Let me just tell you the last incident that happened to me: a few weeks ago I entered a grocery store and I ordered oranges. The salesman asked me: oranges for Jews (juice)? I said yes and he gave me the lousiest oranges in the store! That did it. After that I decided to emigrate to Israel."

*

What is the difference between the right wing of the Israeli Parliament and the right wings of other countries?

The Israeli right wing is not antisemitic.

*

A Jewish father asks a Lebanese Catholic

"What is becoming of your son? What trade is he entering?"

"He will become a priest."

"What? A priest? There is no future in that. You should stop him."

"On the contrary, I believe he has a future. If he does well, he can become a bishop."

"So? I would not consider that a decent career."

"Well, he might even become a cardinal."

"What good is that?"

"The Pope even!"

"I still remain unimpressed."

"What do you think is an admirable position? God?"

"Why not? One of our boys did it!"

*

There had been complaints by several countries that Egypt was shooting down their planes instead of Israeli planes. The Egyptians gave orders that their troops should make sure that a plane was really Israeli before shooting at it. Shortly thereafter a French Concorde was shot down. An investigation was conducted and the troops claimed that it had a Semitic nose !

*

Abraham has a marvelously beautiful wife, Rachel, and his friend Isaac is madly in love with her. One day Isaac cannot resist any longer and he offers her first 500, then 1000 and 2000 dollars if she accepts to receive his favours. For 2000 dollars she capitulates and he receives heavenly satisfaction.

In the evening, Abraham comes home and asks Rachel,

"Did Isaac come to the house this afternoon?"

"Yes, he did."

"I *am* glad because he borrowed 2000 dollars this morning and promised to bring it back to the house this afternoon."

*

A Jew from Israel arrives in New York. He goes to a women's house and asks for a girl called Myriam. He makes love to her and gives her 500 dollars. The girl asks if he will come again. "Yes. I will be back tomorrow." The following day he returns and gives her again 500 dollars. She asks if he will return. "Yes, tomorrow." A third time, the girl receives 500 dollars, but this time he says to her that he will not see her again, for he is returning to Jerusalem. The girl says: "Oh, but I will give you the address of my sister, Sharon, who lives on. . ." He interrupts her: "You don't have to tell me. I know her well. She is the one who gave me the 1500 dollars for you."

*

Israeli poster:

"If you want to visit Egypt, join the Israeli army."

*

What happens to Egyptian girls who forget to take the pill?

They become mummies.

★

A young Israeli boy after school was asked by his father:

"What did you learn today?"

"The rabbi told us how Moses crossed the Red Sea with the chosen people."

"How did he do it?"

"Well, he built a bridge and had his people cross it. Then he placed dynamite at all the pillars, waited until the pursuing Egyptians were on top of it, and then blew it up."

"Is that what the rabbi told you?"

"Not quite. But if I told you his crazy story, you would not believe it."

★

A foreign tourist visits Tel Aviv, accompanied by a Jewish guide. Among the monuments of the city he notices one with the following inscription:

"To Sol Cohen, the unknown soldier." He wonders, astonished:

"That soldier was not unknown, since you knew his name!"

And the guide answers: "No, the inscription is quite correct. Sol Cohen was very well known in Tel Aviv as a jeweller, but no one ever knew him as a soldier."

★

Solution proposed by a citizen for the Middle-East problem: let one party divide the territory and let the other party have the first choice!

★

Wife of Saudi Arabian delegate,

"You bought another Cadillac? Don't we have enough of them?"

"Well, I went into a garage to make a telephone call and I could not leave without buying something."

*

An Arab filled out a US immigration form as follows:
Name: Mohammed Ben Mohammed
Profession: Bodyguard
Sex: enormous

*

The delegate of Saudi Arabia goes to a Cadillac garage and asks, "Do you have your latest model?"

"Yes, but only five cars per customer."

*

A foreigner visits an Arab country after world war II, and after observing the changes which have occurred he says to an Arab friend:

"I just cannot believe the social progress you have made. Before the war all men were riding on camels or mules with their wife walking twelve feet behind. Now I see that the women walk in front. How is that possible?"

Arab: "Now the women walk in front because of the mines."

*

A foreign diplomat asked Begin how the Israelis always managed to win their battles against the enemy. What was the drive behind all their victories?

"It is very simple. We organize the battle line as follows: in the first line we put lawyers. In the second line we put doctors, surgeons, psychiatrists and dentists, and in the third line we put our young men. And you know very well how they all can charge!"

EUROPE

BELGIUM

French President Mendes-France had launched a strong campaign against the drinking habits of the French people. One day, a social worker was talking with a man who was drinking heavily at a cafe bar.

"Don't you know that drinking is terrible for the health of the French people?" (No reaction from the drinking man.)

"Don't you know that 60 per cent of all Frenchmen have severe liver trouble because of alcohol?" (No reaction.)

"Didn't you hear of our President's campaign against alcoholism?"

The drunkard finally looked up and said,

"Yes, I have, but why should I care? I am not a Frenchman, I am Belgian."

*

A Belgian is asked for his opinion on a particular subject. He answers:

"How can I tell you before I have heard what I will say?"

*

Two Belgians were drinking in a bar, talking about love. One said to the other,

"Have you ever heard how Congolese make love?" His friend said no, but heard about it in detail.

When the first Belgian arrived home, he made love with his wife, imitating all the movements his friend had taught him. His wife looked up astonished and asked,

"Why do you suddenly make love like a Congolese?"

*

A Belgian truck manned by a driver and his helper approached an 8-foot tunnel in France — exactly the height of the truck. The driver asked his assistant if he should try going through the tunnel and the aide advised him no because the truck would surely get stuck. The driver, viewing the situation, felt helpless and dismayed. Then a French car stopped, the driver hopped out and asks about the matter. The Belgian explains.

The Frenchman shouted at him:

"You idiot, all you have to do is let some air out of your tires."

The Belgian remains perplexed and retorts:

"But that will not help, because it is not the wheels that scrape. It is the top of the truck."

*

At a cocktail party a gentleman said,

"I am going to tell a Belgian joke."

A lady interjected with, "Oh, be careful, I am Belgian."

"In that case, I will tell it twice."

Lady: "I do not understand you."

*

Retaliatory jokes of the Belgians against the French:

Why do Frenchmen like so much Belgian jokes? Because they are the only ones they can understand.

*

In Belgium it is prohibited to tell jokes on Saturday evenings: people might start laughing the next (Sunday) morning during religious services.

*

A Belgian driver bumped into the back of another car. The policeman said

"Why don't you wash the front window of your car? You can barely see through it."

"It would not help, I left my glasses at home."

*

Belgian husband: "I don't know where I put my pencil."

Wife: "You put it behind your ear."

"Which one? The right or the left?"

*

A Belgian had his two ears badly burnt. A friend asked him how it happened.

"Well, I was ironing my pants when the telephone suddenly rang. By mistake I put the hot iron on my ear."

"How come that your other ear is burnt?"

"Well, I had to call the doctor!"

*

The fog was so dense in France that a Belgian driver decided to play it safe and follow the taillight of a car ahead of him. After a few miles, the other car stopped and he crashed into it.

"Why didn't you signal?" the Belgian asked the Frenchman.

"Why should I?" came the answer. "I am in my own garage."

*

A Belgian lady out driving had a flat tire. She stopped, got out and wrung her hands, lamenting she did not know what to do. Then a truck driver stopped, jacked up the car and changed the tire and the lady said,

"Could you do me one more favour? Please let down the car very gently. My husband is sleeping in the back seat."

*

A Belgian goes to a hardware store and buys ten boxes of mothballs.

Merchant: "My God, your house must be infested with moths."

"No, but it is very hard to hit them with the balls."

*

Guest in a family:

"How come you let your children hammer nails into the dining room table?"

"Oh, I buy the nails wholesale!"

*

Two fellows were chatting in a bar.

"Have you heard the latest Belgian joke?" asked the first man.

"No. But before you tell it, I want you to know that I am Belgian."

"Oh! In that case I will tell it very slowly."

*

CZECHOSLOVAKIA

The President of Czechoslovakia, Novotny, was a former locksmith. One day he noticed that the lock to his office needed repair and he asked for a locksmith. The man arrived and fumbled with the lock for an interminable time, rendering Novotny extremely nervous. Finally, the President could not hold it any longer, and he shouted to the man:

"What is the matter with you? To repair a lock like that would not take me more than ten minutes. You have been here for more than an hour and still you are not finished."

Locksmith: "Yes, but you are a locksmith, and I am a lawyer!"

*

A Czechoslovak peasant walks on a country road towards his village. He kicks a bottle lying on the roadside and a genie pops out of it. The giant says to the peasant: "Since you freed me, you are entitled to three wishes."

The peasant thinks for a while and formulates his first wish:

"I wish the Chinese troops came to Czechoslovakia and then returned home."

"And what is your second wish?"

"I wish the Chinese troops came to Czechoslovakia and returned home."

"And what is your third wish?"

"My third one is that the Chinese troops would come to Czechoslovakia and return home."

Genie: "I will see what I can do, but to tell you the truth, I cannot really understand why you repeated three times the same wish."

Peasant: "Oh, yes. It would mean that the Chinese troops would have to cross the Soviet Union six times!"

*

A Czech citizen is bending over the Karl's bridge in Prag counting, "five, five, five."

A Russian soldier passes by and asks him what he is doing but the Czech does not reply but continues to watch the river intently counting, "five, five, five." The Russian soldier bends over the bridge's railing to see what is going on in the water and the Czech pushes him into the river counting, "six, six, six."

*

The police of Prag finds an old Jew who has been living in the city for many years without being registered with the authorities. They submit him to close interrogation and want to know everything about him. Among others they ask him:

"Do you have a family?"

"Yes, I have an older brother."

"Where does he live?"

"In the Soviet Union."

"What is he doing?"

"He is building socialism."

"Excellent. Do you have any other relatives?"

"Yes, I have a younger brother."

"Is he also living in the Soviet Union?"

"No, he lives in Israel."

"What does he do? Is he also building socialism?"

"Are you kidding? Why should he? It is his own country!"

*

An American businessman visits a Czechoslovakian restaurant for luncheon. The Czech waiter greets him,

"Sir, you are in a centrally planned economy. Our system is perfect. We can offer you any dish your heart desires, provided you pay in dollars." The businessman thinks for a while then says,

"Well, if that is so, I would like to order a dish which I have been craving for all my life: fried elephant ears with little onions."

The waiter rushes to the kitchen and talks to the cook; they see no other way than to notify the central committee of the Communist Party. The central committee feels that communism cannot lose face and they order an elephant to be taken out of the zoo.

The American, sitting near a window, sees an elephant pass by followed by the waiter with an utterly disappointed face.

"Sir, we greatly regret being unable to serve you the dish you requested. We apologize most sincerely and confess that not everything is perfect in our system."

"But how can that be? I just saw an elephant brought to the restaurant!".

"You are right. We have an elephant in Czechoslovakia, but we don't have any little onions!"

*

A Czechoslovakian soldier reports to his officer that a Swiss soldier has stolen his Russian watch. The astonished officer retorts, "You mean to say that a Russian soldier stole your Swiss watch?"

"You said it, Lieutenant, not I."

*

Two Czechs meet in the streets of Prag and comment on the hardness of the times:

"I cannot find any work to do with my two hands."

"This is astonishing. With some effort you should be able to find employment easily in our socialist, planned economy."

"Alas, no, because I am fingerprinted by all the police in the country."

*

A Czech point of view:

"What is the difference between Czechoslovakia and Israel?"

"?"

"Israel is much luckier than Czechoslovakia: it is surrounded by enemies instead of friends."

A Czech citizen goes to a hardware store and asks for a product which would help him get rid of mice.

"My home is infested with rodents. I have tried poison, mousetraps, etc. but nothing has worked. They continue to live and to multiply."

Hardware clerk: "I have something sensational; it is a little mechanical mouse. All you have to do is wind it up, open the door of your house, point its nose towards the door and all mice will follow it and leave your dwelling for ever."

A week later, the customer returns to the hardware store.

"Were you satisfied?" asks the hardwareman.

"Yes, very much so. I first made the little mechanical mouse turn around in the house and all the mice came out of their holes and followed it in circles. Then I pointed its nose towards the door which I opened and all mice left my house for ever."

"So, is there anything else I can do for you?"

"Yes, as a matter of fact there is. I came back to ask if by any chance you sell a little mechanical communist."

*

During the leadership of Leonid Brejnev, the Cathedral of Saint Stefan in Prag received a communication from the Kremlin requesting that the name of the cathedral be changed to Saint Leonid.

The Cathedral's response that they had checked all lists of saints and martyrs but could not find any Saint Leonid was countered by the Kremlin that the suggestion was made to honor Leonid Brejnev and to reinforce the friendship between the Soviet Union and Czechoslovakia. Consequently, the Cathedral wrote back:

"We gladly agree with your proposal. Please send us his bones."

*

Remark of a Czechoslovak housewife:

"We have such a perfectly planned economy in Czechoslovakia that when there is no ham, there are no eggs either."

*

At 4 o'clock in the morning a Prag apartment superintendent dashed through the building knocking at the tenants doors.

"Get up quickly. But don't worry: it is only a fire."

*

Czechoslovak riddle:
Are Russians friends or brothers?
Brothers, because friends one can choose.

*

Dubcek arrives in heaven together with Brejnev and Mao Tse Tung.

St. Peter tells them that each of them can have one wish.

Brejnev: "I wish an earthquake would shake China and wipe out its entire population."

Mao Tse Tung: "I wish all the atomic bombs stored in Russia exploded and transformed the country into a vast desert."

St. Peter turns to Dubcek:

"And what is your wish?"

"Well, I simply wish that you fulfill the wishes of those two gentlemen."

*

A Czech who has lost his voice, instead of going to the doctor, goes to the secret police and writes on a pad of paper:

"I have lost my voice."

Police: "Don't worry. We will make you talk."

*

A foreign diplomat once asked a Czech official,

"While studying the organization chart of your government, I was surprised to learn that you had a

Ministry of the Navy. How can that be, since you have no access to the seas?"

"Well, if the USSR has a Ministry of Justice, why can't we have a Ministry of the Navy?"

*

The President of Czechoslovakia, at an audience with the Pope, asks the Holy Pontiff how his country can get rid of the Soviet troops. The Pope suggests two ways:

"The first and natural way would be force, using all the men and arms at your disposal."

"Well, this would be very difficult and would cause a bloodbath. I would prefer if they withdrew voluntarily."

"That is the second way, namely the supernatural one."

*

A Czech citizen was condemned to 15 years of prison for having called a minister an idiot. A foreign correspondent asked why the verdict was so severe; usually the sentence for personal insults was no more than one year.

"He was not condemned for insults. He was convicted for revealing a state secret."

*

FEDERAL REPUBLIC OF GERMANY

Promising that he will not start any trouble, Hitler asks God for a week's leave on Earth, and God grants him his request.

Hitler returns within a day. Surprised, God asks him, "What went wrong?"

"I could not stand it. Everything is upside down on Earth. Can you imagine: the Jews are now waging war and the Germans are making money!"

*

Hitler often blew his top against the Jews. One day he did it in front of Hjalmar Schacht, his Minister of Finance who said to him:

"Fuhrer, the truth is that these people are more intelligent than the Germans. Do you want me to prove it?"

"Alright", said Hitler. "You try."

And Schacht took Hitler for a shopping spree in the streets of Berlin. They entered into a Chinaware store and Schacht asked if they had a tea-set for left-handed people. The German shopkeeper looked at him arrogantly and said:

"Obviously not. We do not carry such things."

Then they went into a Jewish shop and Schacht asked the same question. The Jewish shopkeeper said:

"Let me see. If you wait a moment, I think I happen to have one set left in my backstore. Of course, it will cost you more, because it is a very unusual set."

After a while he came back with six saucers and cups which he placed in front of the two, with the handles turned to the left.

Schacht bought the set and when they left the store he said to Hitler:

"You see, as I told you, these people are infinitely more intelligent than the average German."

But Hitler blew his top and shouted:

"Yes, but they are always lucky. This chap just happened to have such a set, while the German did not."

*

A French woman, her son, a Prussian, and a Bavarian were riding in the same train compartment in Germany. The Prussian mumbled disparaging remarks at the woman because she was speaking French to her son. The Bavarian after a while blew his top and shouted at the Prussian,

"Haven't you ever heard of world brotherhood and reconciliation between nations, you damned Prussian?"

*

A little boy was playing on a beach in North Germany: For the first time in his life he saw a naked little girl and he asked his mother:

"Mother, why does not this little girl have what I have?"

Mother: "Oh! she is a little refugee from East Germany and, you know, these people have lost everything!"

*

During a bombardment of the city of Koln, Thinnes was looking for his friend Scheel all over the apartment house where they both lived. He finds him in the attic, his head sticking out of the roof; he wears a helmet and carries an old gun. All around him projectors scan the sky and bombs rain over the city. Thinnes begs his friend to come to the cellar, but Scheel retorts:

"This is the safest place in town. If you read the official communiques, you know that military targets are never hit!"

*

A German peasant was visiting the Ministry of Agriculture in Berlin during Hitler's reign. In a waiting room he saw a globe of the world and he asked an official what the different colours meant.

"The vast blue areas are the seas and oceans. The red area represents the Soviet Union, the brown the United States, and the yellow patch China."

"And where is Germany?" The official took a pin and pointed at a tiny grey spot. The astonished peasant gasped, "Does Hitler know that?"

*

Johann and Ludwig van Beethoven were never on good terms. On a New Year's Day, Johann the businessman who had just acquired a large piece of land sent his brother a card which he signed: Johann van Beethoven, land-owner. The composer sent it back, signed: Ludwig van Beethoven, brain-owner.

*

A German husband who had been "cheating on" his wife all his life died. Out of revenge, she had him interred naked in his coffin, since this had been his preferred state while alive.

A few days later she felt remorse and decided to have him disinterred and dressed decently. But the coffin was empty and in it she found this note:

"I have moved a few tombs further to Frau Schmidt."

*

A German furniture dealer went to Paris to have a good time. He went to a famous nightclub where he was told he would encounter adventure. He invited a beautiful French woman to have a drink with him. She accepted, but she didn't know any German and he didn't know any French. On a napkin he drew the picture of a table with two plates on it. She understood that he wanted to invite her for dinner. He took her to a first-class restaurant on the Champs Elysees. There the two spent the evening together having a conversation through drawings. For instance, he drew a bottle of champagne and she understood immediately. As the night was advancing, she took a piece of paper and drew a bed on it.

The German looked at it, grinning all over his face and said to her, admiringly:

"How on Earth did you guess that I was a furniture dealer?"

*

A famous German composer used to drink too much with his friends. He lived in a row of houses which were all the same and would have had difficulty in finding his home if he had not used a very simple device. He kicked every metal footscraper at the entrance of each house until he found one that had an E flat sound: Home.

*

Three condemned men were to be guillotined. One was a Frenchman, the second an Englishman, the third a German.

Prior to the execution, the Frenchman was asked if he had a last wish: "Yes, I would like to make love a last time." His wish was granted. When he came back, his head was placed on the guillotine, the blade was released but it stopped a few millimeters from his neck.

According to French law, the sentence was considered executed and he went free.

The Englishman's last wish was to attend a religious service. When he came back, the same thing happened again: the blade stopped short of his neck and he was released.

When the German was asked for his last wish, he turned to the executioner and said: "I would like you to lubricate that blade and have it in perfect operating condition. I cannot stand such sloppiness."

*

Conversation between two Germans:

"Do you know that the next President of the United States will be a Jew?"

"This is hard to believe. What makes you think so?"

"Well, nach dem Regen (Reagan) kommt der Sonnenshein. (After the rain comes sunshine.)

*

FRANCE

Two French noblemen leave for the Crusades.

"Oh, God!" says one. "I forgot to lock my wife's chastity-belt! Could you wait for me; I will be back shortly."

When he returns, forward they go. After a while the other nobleman ventures:

"I cannot help wondering why you returned to lock your wife's chastity belt. She does not strike me as one who would attract many men, on the contrary."

"I know that all too well," answered the first knight. "I went back to lock her belt so that after the Crusades, when I return, I can say that I lost the key!"

*

A French nobleman was leaving his castle for the Crusades. He locked his young wife's chastity belt, and gave the key to his most trusted friend and said,

"If in seven years I am not back, it will mean that I am dead and I want you then to unlock her belt and give her the freedom to choose and marry another man."

Barely an hour after he had left the castle, he heard the sound of a galloping horse behind him. It was his trusted friend.

"I am sorry, but you gave me the wrong key!"

*

A French movie star was living near the military academy of St. Cyr not far from Paris. She was known to be of the amorous type, but she charged the equivalent of a thousand dollars per night.

The cadets finally decided to organize a lottery, selling tickets for five dollars, the prize being 1000 dollars.

The winning cadet knocked at her door and was admitted upon payment of the thousand dollars. They spent the night together and the following morning she asked the young man how he could dispose of such a substantial sum of money. He told her the story, whereupon the star said to him:

"Young man, that is very nice. As a matter of fact, the night we spent together will be free for you; here are your five dollars."

*

No Frenchman ever died of modesty.

*

A French father once took his little son to the Louvre Museum in Paris. When they came to the statue of the Venus of Milo, he said to the boy,

"You see. This is what will happen to you, if you continue biting your fingernails!"

*

A young foreigner wanted to join Napoleon's army, but he did not know any French. An aide to the Emperor said to him,

"Do not worry. The Emperor always asks the same three questions: 1. How old are you? 2. How long have you been in France? 3. Do you want to be paid in cash or in kind? To the first question you answer 25; to the second 5; and to the third both."

But Napoleon changed the order of his questions and asked:

"How long have you been in France?"

"Twenty-five years."

"How old are you?"

"Five years."

Astonished, the Emperor asked:

"Are you crazy or am I?"

Recruit: "Both."

*

An old French lady had a male cat whom she loved dearly. But the animal was a loafer and she had him castrated. Then one day as she was cleaning up her attic, she found an old silver lamp which she rubbed to make it shine. A genie came out and told her that she could make three wishes. Her first wish was to become young and beautiful again. Her second wish was that her cat become a handsome young man, and her third wish was that he would fall in love with her. All three wishes were granted, and when the handsome young man stood in front of her, he said, "Now you will regret that you had me castrated!"

*

During the German occupation of France, a German officer, a young Frenchman, a French girl and an old man were travelling in the same train compartment. When the train crossed a tunnel, the sound of a kiss could be heard in the darkness, followed by a resounding slap. When the train emerged from the tunnel, the German officer was rubbing his cheek and the four passengers mused:

Old man: "The German officer must have tried to kiss the young girl and she slapped him in the face."

Young girl: "The German officer must have tried to kiss me, but he kissed the young man who slapped him back."

German officer: "The young Frenchman must have tried to kiss the girl. She wanted to hit him, but by mistake she hit me."

Young Frenchman: "Isn't it a shame that I had to kiss my own hand in order to slap a German officer in the face!"

*

An elderly French peasant woman in confession says to the priest,

"I cheated on my husband and made love with another man."

"When was this?" asks the priest.

"Thirty years ago."

"Well, you don't have to confess that anymore since it was such a long time ago."

"Oh, but I like to talk to someone once in a while about it."

*

The son of an American diplomat in Paris asks his father what "inflation" means.

The father answers that it means a general price increase.

"What difference does it make?" comments the boy.

"Well, I would put it as follows: Before inflation, here in Paris, life meant for me wine, restaurants and women. Since inflation it means beer, dining at home and your mother."

*

Once the municipality of Paris ordered a patriotic monument from the famous sculptor Maillol. Maillol thought it over for a moment.

"I see. Something symobolizing the French Republic. What you have in mind then is an attractive woman's behind."

*

A young French female asks a gentleman in the Paris subway to give her his seat which is marked: "For pregnant women." The gentleman obliges but examines the girl attentively.

She does not show any sign of pregnancy. Her abdomen is flat like a board. So he asks her:

"How many months have you been pregnant, Miss?"

"Oh, it just happened an hour ago, but it emptied me of all my strength. I had to sit down, because I feel as if my feet had been cut off!"

*

After the second world war, during the third French Republic, political parties in France were so numerous from the extreme left to the extreme right, that it was impossible to find a name for a new party. One day, however, a French Parliamentarian had a brilliant idea: he founded the "extreme center" party!

*

The French police once came upon a foreigner who had lived in France for more than twenty years without a permit or registration. They asked him how this was possible:

He said: "Well, when I arrived in your country, I called the Immigration Office and a girl on the telephone said to me: Ne quittez pas (do not leave: the French equivalent for hold on), which I did."

*

Two men stand next to each other in a Paris sidewalk men's room. One says to the other,

"You must be an Alsation Jew."

"Yes, I am. How did you know?"

"You come from the village of Gundelsheim."

"Yes, indeed, that is my hometown."

"And you were born between 1930 and 1935."

"Correct again. This is amazing. How did you know?"

"Well, I knew a Rabbi Kaplan who lived in that village between 1930 and 1935. He used to circumcise all kids diagonally, and you have been urinating against me for the last three minutes!"

*

During World War II the people of Alsace-Lorraine were fined 50 pfennig by the German police when they were caught speaking French. The standard joke was to hand the policeman a one mark bill and to say:

"Keep the change. Au-revoir."

*

When Robert Schuman was Minister of Foreign Affairs of France, a book appeared in which a former French diplomat accused his country's foreign service of being a refuge for homosexuals. Schuman asked one of his personal assistants to make a discreet investigation and the aide reported back to him.

"There are exactly 23 gays in the French foreign service, including Paris and all French missions abroad."

Schuman, pensive, commented:

"This is a rather low figure. As a matter of fact, it is identical to the number which was given to me by the Director of Personnel of the Ministry."

Suddenly his face lit up and with a candid smile he asked his aide:

"Oh, but are you sure that they are the same 23!"

*

An Irishman visiting Paris went to a cheap hotel where the landlady asked if he wanted a blonde, brunette or redheaded woman at his service.

"Will this cost a lot of money?"

"No, not at all. It will be entirely free."

When the Irishman left the hotel, he did not have to pay for the woman or room, and was given a sum of 500 francs.

Back in Ireland he told the story to his best friend who rushed to Paris the following weekend to the same hotel. He got the same offer — a blonde, brunette or a redhead; and when he left he didn't have to pay either but was given a sum of 1000 francs. He asked why he received a higher sum than his friend,

"Well, it is quite natural; we only took pictures of your friend, but you were on television."

*

Dupont returns home with his twelve year old son Toto after having had him examined by a psychiatrist. He says to his wife:

"Darling, Toto has been declared totally sound and normal. The nurse showed him an electric train, a puzzle, building blocks, and a chemistry set, and the psychiatrist asked him with which toy he wanted to play. He answered: "The nurse!"

*

Little Toto asks his father:

"Dad, is it true that the stork brings babies?"

"Yes, son."

"Is it true that Santa Claus brings the toys at Christmas?"

"Correct you are."

"And is it true that God places the bread and the food on our table?"

"It is a fact, son."

"Well, then, father, could you tell me what you are doing?"

*

During World War I German soldiers used to raise above their trenches a sign boasting:

"Gott mit Uns." (God with us.)

The Americans in their trenches decided to raise their own sign saying:

"We Got Mittens Too."

*

During World War II a little French boy asked a German soldier what was written on his buckle.

German soldier: "Gott mit uns. God is on our side."

Little boy: "That is nothing. We are much better off: we have the Americans with us."

*

Dupont was intimate with his wife one evening. Little Toto, their son, hears his mother moan. The following morning he asks his father what was wrong with her. "Oh, it was nothing. She had a stomach ache."

In the evening, when father returns home from work, little Toto says to him:

"Dad, Mom had again two stomach aches today: the first time was when the mailman came and the second time when uncle Albert visited her."

*

Little Jacques asks his grandmother,

"Grandma, how was I born?"

"You were born from a cabbage."

"And how was my little sister born?"

"She was also born from a cabbage."

"And my father?"

"From a cabbage too, of course."

Jacques looks at his grandmother in utter bewilderment.

"Doesn't anyone make love normally in our family?"

*

The coal miners of Lorraine are on strike to obtain a salary increase. They send a delegation of black-faced workers to President de Gaulle in Paris. The General inquires about their grievances:

"Mon General, we want 15 francs an hour, but the government is prepared to pay us only ten."

The General reflects for a moment and then decrees:

"You shall be paid twelve francs fifty."

The coal miners leave satisfied and deGaulle turns to one of his aides:

"By the way, could you tell me from which African country these gentlemen were?"

*

General de Gaulle was travelling by boat to Latin America where he was to visit several heads of state. As he was working on his first speech in his cabin, he realized that he had forgotten the name of the President of Venezuela. He sent the following cable to his Minister of Foreign Affairs, Couve de Murville:

"Do you know the name of the President of Venezuela?"

"Yes."

Infuriated, de Gaulle cabled back: "Yes, who?"

Couve de Murville answered:

"Yes, my General."

*

To a young man who was going to work with General de Gaulle, an old friend of the General said:

"It is very easy to work with the President. All you have to do is to say 'Yes, my General' if you agree with him and 'All right, my General' when you disagree."

*

A customer asks a little French girl in a bistro to put some water into his wine.

She answers, "Oh, there is no need. My mother put a lot of it in the barrel this morning."

*

De Gaulle was visiting the Louvre museum with his wife.

He commented on several paintings, each time mistaking either the subject or the artist. His wife patiently and gently corrected him. Finally, he stopped in front of the image of a tall squire and exclaimed,

"This time I cannot be wrong. It is Don Quixote by Velazquez."

"I am sorry, darling, but you are wrong again. You are standing in front of a mirror."

*

When de Gaulle left the Presidency, a friend asked him where he wanted to be buried at death, suggesting burial next to Napoleon at the Invalides.

De Gaulle responded: "Are you out of your mind to think that I would ever accept burial next to that small Corsican corporal?"

"You might perhaps wish to be buried under the Arc de Triomphe?"

"And you must be joking! I could not stand all those American tourists hanging around all day long."

"Well, then, how about being buried next to Joan of Arc?"

"That is a fine idea. I believe that she would be worthy of it."

*

Napoleon used to say: "Soldiers, I am satisfied with you."

De Gaulle said: "Soldiers, I am satisfied with myself."

*

De Gaulle was in his bathtub when his wife Yvonne inadvertently entered the bathroom. "Oh, my God," she exclaimed.

"My dear, in private you may call me Charles."

*

De Gaulle was so conceited that on his birthdays he sent telegrams of congratulations to his mother.

*

A French farmer shows his farm and garden to visitors. When they arrive at the orchard, he points to a tree and says: "This is the Freedom Tree."

"Did you plant it at the Liberation, when the Nazis left?"

"No, it is the tree on which my wife hanged herself."

*

Jacque's mother and father lock themselves up in the bedroom one Saturday evening. When the father emerges, little Jacque asks him,

"What did you do in there, locked up with mother?"

"We ordered a little sister for you."

"Are you tired?"

"Why?"

"Because, if you aren't, you could also order me a bicycle."

*

A woman was lying in an empty space between two cars along a sidewalk in Paris. A policeman came running and asked her,

"What is the matter? Are you hurt, Madam?"

"No. I am just reserving this parking place for my husband."

*

After the first meeting between the new French President Mitterand and German President Schmidt, the former was called: "Schmitterand."

*

Three Frenchmen arrive late in the evening at a railroad station and ask the stationmaster,

"When does the next train for X leave?"

"In an hour."

So, the three fellows go to a nearby bar. An hour later they arrive at the platform just as the train is leaving. They ask when the next train leaves and are told in an hour. So they return to the bar and get increasingly drunk. The stationmaster warns them finally that the last train leaves at midnight.

Just at midnight they come running as the train pulls out of the station. Two of them are able to jump it, but the third, a rather plump fellow, cannot make it. He remains on the platform, laughing his head off. The stationmaster asks him what is so funny.

"I was supposed to take that train. My two friends were only accompanying me to the station!"

*

An American visiting Paris asked his guide when he saw the Arch of Triumph:

"Is that General de Gaulle's sentry-box?"

*

GERMAN DEMOCRATIC REPUBLIC

Three East Germans are in the same prison cell telling each other the circumstances of their arrests.

"I am accused of sabotage, because I arrived late at the factory. But it was not my fault: my lousy watch is always slow."

"I was accused of espionage, because my watch is fast and I arrived a few minutes early at the factory."

"My watch is always accurate, and I am accused of having bought it in the West."

*

An East German visits a psychiatrist:

"Doctor, you must help me. I am going out of my mind. Every night I dream that I am crossing the Berlin wall."

Psychiatrist: "This is nothing unusual. As a matter of fact, I can tell you confidentially that many of our compatriots have the same dream."

"I know. But in my case it is worse: I dream that I am crossing it from West to East!"

*

Two dogs meet in West Berlin. One is from the West, the other from the East.

Western dog: "How do they treat you in your socialist country?"

Eastern dog: "Extremely well. I have a warm, comfortable doghouse, a soft feather cushion, delicious natural food and not any of those horrible American cans, I can swim in clean unpolluted rivers and I do not risk being run over by so many cars. I have it really good there."

Western dog: "Why then do you come to West Berlin?"

Eastern dog: "I come here to bark."

*

A customer in East Berlin wants to buy new tires for his car but is told,

"There are none available here; there are some in Rostock. Here is a train ticket."

"That train ticket takes me only half way to Rostock!"

"Well, this is where the line of people starts."

*

East and West Germany have divided Karl Marx between themselves:

East Germany has the Manifesto.

West Germany has Das Kapital.

*

All of humanity had been destroyed by an atomic war, except for three archaeologists who were deep in an archaeological cave in Africa: a French woman, an American woman and an East German male. Emerging from the cave they began to resume life in their camp. Several weeks passed and the women became increasingly nervous. Yet the East German did not make any advances. Finally, the two women decided to talk to him.

"We cannot go on like this. We are the only lucky survivors. Our duty is to procreate — to start the human story again."

The East German looked at them sternly:

"All right, I am prepared to do my duty, but I have one condition."

"What is it?"

"You must both first recognize East Germany."

*

Sign in East Berlin:

"You are now in the free zone of Berlin.
It is forbidden to take pictures."

*

An East German is accused of having smuggled western matches into East Germany. His defense was that he needed them to light the Soviet matches sold in East Germany.

*

A high East German party official visits an asylum. The inmates have assembled in his honour and are singing a song about the greatness of the communist revolution. One of them is not singing, and the party official asks him why not.

"Because I am not crazy; I am a doctor."

*

The President of the German Democratic Republic wanted to take a vacation abroad, so he turned to Helmut Schmidt, Chancellor of West Germany, to stand in for him. Before leaving he said,

"We have three fundamental problems here: lack of housing, lack of food and too many people going to church."

When he returned from vacation two weeks later, he was astonished to see signs on many buildings: "Apartment for rent." There were no lines in front of foodstores and churches were empty. He asked Schmidt how he had achieved that miracle.

"It was very simple. First we opened the border to the West and many people left, thus leaving many apartments for rent. Then we closed the USSR border and as a result the food stopped leaving the country. Finally we announced that all church sermons would be delivered by leaders of the Communist party."

*

HUNGARY

Two Hungarians commenting on the day's events:

"Aren't you glad that the price of bread went down?"

"What? I haven't heard that. On the contrary, all prices are going up."

"Well, it all depends how you look at it. For instance, today they increased the price of telephone calls by a hundred percent. That means that for the price of one telephone call you can now buy two loaves of bread. Consequently the price of bread went down!"

*

A Hungarian goes to a post office in Budapest and complains that the postage stamps picturing a national leader do not stick. The postal clerk is skeptical; in his view socialist stamps are as good as capitalist ones, if not better. Nevertheless he will have them inspected.

A week later, the postal clerk has his report, and when the customer comes back, he says to him:

"These stamps are of perfect quality. If they don't stick, it must be your fault. Could you show me how you use them?"

The customer shows him and the employee exclaims:

"Of course they don't stick! You are spitting on the wrong side!"

*

A foreign journalist interviewing the President of Hungary notices that there are several telephones on the official's desk but none of them has a part into which you can talk. He expresses surprise, and the President says,

"These telephones are directly linked with Moscow. I can listen to what they say, but I cannot talk back."

*

Grun and Cohen meet in hell.

Grun: "How have you been? I have not seen you for a long time. What are you doing?"

Cohen: "Oh! I am in the capitalist hell. My job is to carry buckets of water from a distant well to a hole which never fills up. It is an excruciating and monotonous job. I am forced to do it from morning to evening, day after day, without any rest. It is really hell. And how about you?"

Grun: "I am in the communist hell. As a matter of fact I have the same punishment as you: I am to carry water in a bucket from a well to a distant pond. But I cannot complain. I have a rather easy life: one day there is no water, the other day there is no bucket, and when the two happen to be available, it usually is a communist holiday!"

*

A Hungarian has committed a serious political offense. He is condemned to five years of prison, to be followed by expulsion from the country. The judge asks him if he has any comments:

"Yes, your Honour. Could I not start with the expulsion?"

"What is COMECON?" asked a Hungarian to a UN expert who was visiting the country.

"It is the Central Organ for Mutual Economic Cooperation among Communist nations."

"No, not at all. I will explain it to you. You see, here in Hungary we are producing little dwarfs made of clay, groups such as Snow-White and the Seven Dwarfs, which are placed in gardens for decoration. Well, we export these dwarfs to Bulgaria which in return sends us little chicks. These chicks we feed with our good Hungarian grain until they become big poultry. That poultry we export to Czechoslovakia which in return sends us little piglets. These piglets we feed with our good Hungarian corn until they become big, fat pigs. These pigs we export to Romania against little calves. These calves we feed with our good Hungarian grain until they become big cows and oxen. And these cows and oxen we export to the Soviet Union. . . which in return sends us the clay to make the little dwarfs!"

*

A young Hungarian visits the police in Budapest and asks if he could obtain an exit visa to go and live in the United States.

"Why on earth do you want to live in America" asks the police.

"Because I have an old uncle there who is blind and who needs care. I happen to be his only relative."

"Is your uncle wealthy?"

"Yes. He was a very successful businessman."

"So why don't you suggest to him that he return to Hungary and you take care of him here?"

"I beg your pardon, I said that he was blind, not that he was crazy!"

*

A stupid Hungarian policeman was seen walking arm in arm on the main boulevard of Budapest with a female penguin. The chief of the police gave him hell and ordered him to take the penguin to the zoo. The following day the policeman was seen again walking with the penguin in the main street, and the chief of police, half out of his mind, shouted at him:

"Didn't I tell you to take this penguin to the zoo?"

"Yes and I tried to, but *she* didn't want to. She preferred to go to the movies."

*

IRELAND

There are only three hundred Jews left in Ireland. Most of them are shopkeepers. One day, Irish terrorists blew up the window of one of the Jewish department stores, and the owner came flying out of his store

"Why are you doing that to me? I am a Jew!"

"Are you a Catholic Jew or a Protestant Jew?"

*

The chief of the UN Irish contingent to the Congo advised his troops as follows:

"You are now UN peace soldiers. I don't want you to get into any troubles and brawls. For example, if a Congolese tells you that Africa is bigger than Ireland, I don't want you to have a fight about it."

*

An Irish priest delivers a sermon on sin:

"It all starts with the first cigarette. That cigarette leads to the first glass of whiskey which leads to the first woman."

Male voice from the congregation:

"And where can I buy those terrific cigarettes?"

*

A nasty joke told by Scotsmen about the Irish:

"What corresponds to an IQ of 144?"

"288 Irishmen."

*

An Irish UN staff member writes home to his friend:

"The wonderful thing with those air-conditioned offices at the UN is that you don't have to wait until winter to catch cold."

*

An Irish priest is going over the fields in procession, blessing the earth and sprinkling holy water. He comes to a badly kept field whose owner begs him to be particularly generous with the holy water. The priest replies:

"This field does not need holy water. It needs manure."

*

A priest going to a distant hamlet in Ireland for a christening asks the peasant if he is ready.

"Yes, I smoked the ham and the Mrs. has baked all the cakes."

"I meant are you ready spiritually?"

"Yes, I have ten liters of fifteen-year-old whiskey ready."

*

UN Irish staff member to the doctor:

"My method, when I have a cold, is to stay at home in bed and to open a bottle of whiskey. In two hours it is finished."

"Your cold?"

"No, the bottle of whiskey."

*

A New York Irishman was looking for a manual job at the UN. The foreman looked him up and down, and asked:

"Are you a mechanic?"

"No, sir. I am a McCarthy."

*

Fifty Englishmen are locked up in a room with one locked door, the key to which is thrown away. One of the Englishmen has an idea how to escape. The other 49 listen, and all escape together.

Fifty Irishmen are imprisoned in the same room. The door is locked and the key thrown away. Every Irishman has a different idea how to escape. They are still imprisoned in the room.

*

Irish saying:

Try to reach heaven at least a half hour before the devil finds out that you are dead.

*

ITALY

Three cardinals cross St. Peter's Square in Rome after a conference on the marriage of priests. One of them asks,

"Do you think that we will ever see this reform during our lifetime?"

Second cardinal: "I do not even believe that our children will see it."

Third cardinal: "Neither will our grandchildren."

*

The Italian soccer team beat the French team against all expectations. The captain of the winning team told the captain of the French team,

"We won, because we prayed to God before the game."

"I cannot understand it, because we prayed to God too."

"Yes, but you prayed in French and not in Italian."

*

There was once a young Italian boy who was an absolute prodigy. He solved the most incredible mathematical problems and answered accurately the most difficult scientific and philosophical questions. Word about him reached the Vatican where a college of Jesuits decided to meet with him and to ask him a number of thorny theological questions.

One of the questions put to the boy was the following:

"When Jesus was born, was he happy or unhappy?"

The little boy answered without a moment of hesitation:

"He was unhappy."

"What makes you say that?"

"Well, when he looked to the right he saw an ox; when he looked at the left he saw an ass, and he commented sadly: Is that the society of Jesus?"

*

An atheist military dictator asks for an audience with the Pope. Surrounded by his cardinals, His Holiness receives him. When the visitor arrives, the Pope steps down from his throne, walks towards him and kisses his hand.

After the audience, the irate cardinals blow their top. How could the Pope kiss the hand of a renowned godless dictator?

The Pope explains his behaviour thus,

"When I saw him arrive, I had suddenly a vision; I saw a resemblance to the Messiah: he was born in a stable; he was raised amongst animals and there are crowds of people who are anxiously awaiting his crucifixion."

*

Italian guide: "When the Tower of Pisa leans to the right, it means that it will rain."

And when it leans to the left?

"It means that you come from the other side of the street."

*

U Thant liked to tell this story which was related to him by young King Paul of Greece who was exiled to Italy.

The King who lived in the Roman Campagna liked to jog around the countryside for long hours. One day he rested at the fence of a farmhouse and engaged in a conversation with the peasant who was tilling his garden. After a while, when the young King was about to leave, the peasant asked him:

"You are a nice young man. Who are you? What is your name?"

The King answered: "I am King Paul of Greece."

Whereupon the peasant had a broad grin, shrugged his shoulders and commented:

"I io sono Napoleone!" And I am Napoleon!

*

An Italian worker precedes the holy procession through the village waving a big red communist banner.

A bystander asks him:

"Why do you do that?"

"I do it in honour of the Madonna and out of love for her."

*

Italian schoolteacher mentioned to another,

"Isn't it strange that our congressmen always vote more funds for prisons than for schools?"

"It is probably because they know that they will never return to school."

*

Italians describe government as having one long arm and one short arm. The long arm is to take away money from the people, the short arm is to hand it out to those who are close to power.

*

After the election of each Pope, it is customary for the chief rabbi in Rome to pay a visit to the new Pontiff and to present him with a small, hermetically closed box. The Pope, each time, is supposed to return the box without opening it.

When Pope John Paul II was elected and the rabbi paid him the traditional visit, he said,

"Let us open the box. I am dying to see what is in it."

They opened it and found a very old parchment bearing a text in a language they could not understand. The Pope called in one of his linguistic experts who said to him,

"The text is in Aramaic, the language which was spoken when Jesus lived."

"Can you read it?"

"Yes."

"What does it say?"

"It is the bill for the Last Supper!"

*

A Bishop visits an Italian village. He complains that the bells did not ring when he arrived. The priest and the parish council give him ten different reasons, except the real one: that the village had no bells.

*

During World War I an Italian lieutenant lined up his infantrymen in a trench facing the enemy lines. Looking at his watch he said to them:

"At one o'clock sharp, I will shout "Avanti" and everybody will jump out of the trench and start the attack."

He did as he said. When it was exactly one o'clock he rushed out of the trench shouting Avanti. Then he turned around and saw that nobody was following him. Instead, the soldiers were standing in the trench, applauding him and chanting:

"Bravissimo, teniente. Que bella voce!"

*

Nero has organized huge circus ceremonies in the Coliseum. Among others, several hundred Christians are being thrown to the lions with Nero himself presiding over the games.

Many Christians are devoured by the wild beasts; then the Emperor notices a group of men and women standing tightly together apart from the lions who dare not touch them. Infuriated, he asks for an explanation.

"Your Majesty, a terrible mistake has been made: these people are not Christians; they are Christian Democrats!"

*

The Italian Minister of the Interior visits a convent. The nuns beg him for some money for the roof is leaking, the equipment is antiquated, and the heating system is out of order. The Minister says that he will study the case and give it consideration.

Next he visits a prison where the inmates ask him for a swimming pool, a tennis court, a game room and many other amenities. The Minister agrees immediately. When he leaves the prison, his assistant asks him why he was so hard with the sisters and so generous with the prisoners.

"It is simple: we will never live in that convent, but we might someday be inmates of that prison."

*

Three Italians go to see a psychiatrist. The professional asks the first of them, "What is wrong with you?"

"I think I am Napoleon"

"Who told you so?"

"My mother." He turns to the second man,

"And what is wrong with you?"

"I think I am Napoleon."

"Who told you?"

"God!" At that point, the third Italian vehemently protests,

"I never told him that he was Napoleon!"

*

The Italian army was to launch a large attack during World War II. Mussolini told the soldiers that he would himself give the order for the attack: he would fly over the front and drop a feather from the plane. When the feather reached the ground, the attack would begin. But after he threw the feather, nothing happened and he returned to the front to see what was going on. There he saw all the men standing in the open and blowing the feather up as it tried to reach the ground.

*

NORDIC COUNTRIES

In a barren part of Norway a peasant decided to improve a rocky, infertile patch of land. After years of hard work the field became productive and yielded a good harvest. The pastor of the village decided to go and have a look. He found the peasant working there and he commented to him,

"This is now a mighty fine field. You must be grateful to God, the owner of all things."

"Yes, but you should have seen it when God was the sole owner!"

*

A Swede was invited over to Denmark to have a drinking party with a Danish friend.

They sat down in front of a large bottle of aquavit and began to drink. Each time the Swede lifted his glass to his lips, he said Skol.

After a while the Dane snapped back at him,

"Look, did you come here to drink or to talk?"

*

President Kekkonen of Finland was the guest of President Brejnev in Moscow. At dinner, Mr. Brejnev said to him,

"The relations between our two countries are just perfect. I cannot visualize a single problem between us. In every respect, be it political, economic or cultural, Soviet-Finnish relations are ideal. As a matter of fact they are so good that a thought has occurred to me. Why don't we make a last step and merge our two countries? What do you think?"

"Let me think it over during the night."

The following morning, at breakfast, Brejnev asked Kekkonen,

"Well, how do you feel about my proposal?"

"I thought a lot about it and have come to the conclusion that it is a bad idea."

"Why?"

"Because I really don't feel inclined to run such a big country."

*

No trees are allowed to be felled near the border between Finland and the USSR, for fear that a worker might be hit by a falling tree and might call for help, in which case the Russians would come.

*

A young Finn was sitting next to a young girl in a bus in Helsinki. The girl greeted him nicely and he likewise.

"Nice weather today." He nodded his head.

When the bus stopped, the two got out and walked together. The girl tried

"Where do you work? Do you still go to school?" The young man stopped, looked at her and said,

"Could we sit down on a bench and kiss. The talking and flirting has lasted long enough."

*

A newly recruited young nun arrived in a Finnish convent where no talking was allowed. After her first year, the Mother Superior permitted her to say one sentence.

"My bed is too hard." A year later she was again allowed to say one sentence.

"I don't like the food." The third year, she said,

"It is too cold during the winter."

At that point, the Mother Superior snapped back,

"You are expelled; since you have joined our community you have done nothing but complain and talk."

*

Tuomioja, the Finnish mediator and UN diplomat, was known for his astonishing capacity to remain silent. Once he told the following story to explain his attitude.

A woodcutter who lived deep in the woods of Finland had a son who didn't talk. Years passed and the father was desperate to help his mute son. One day, as they were cutting trees in the woods, a bear came from behind and was about to attack the father, when the son shouted,

"Father beware, there is a bear behind you."

The father turned around and killed the bear with his axe.

As they walked happily home, the father said,

"Son, not only am I grateful to you for having saved my life, but this is the happiest day for me because I now discover that you know how to talk. But tell me, son. Why did you never talk before?"

"Because I had nothing important to say."

*

To a colleague who could not understand his muteness, Tuomioja once answered:

"The advantage of remaining silent is that you don't have to explain what you have not said."

*

One day a woman who was sitting next to Tuomioja at a diplomatic dinner said to him,

"Mr. Executive Secretary, I have bet that I would make you say more than five words."

Tuomioja turned to her with a smile and said,

"You lost."

*

A salesman visits the shop of a customer in Helsinki. The proprietor is not in, and a Finnish sales girl recently arrived from the countryside tends the shop.

"Is the boss not in?"

"No, the boss is not in."

"Will he be in soon?"

"Yes, he will be in soon."

The salesman reads a newspaper and waits a considerable time. The shopkeeper is still not back.

"Where did the boss go?"

"To Japan, but he will be back soon."

*

A Finn and a Swede decide to go camping together. In the evening while erecting the tent, the Swede comments,

"I think it is going to rain."

"No, I don't think so."

"But look at the sky, those dark , low, fast-running clouds. They are a sure sign that we are going to have a storm."

The Finn begins to pack his things, and the Swede asks him,

"What are you doing? Where are you going?"

"I am quitting. I just cannot stand so much talk."

*

A young Finnish man took his girlfriend for a sleighride in the night. Raptured by the beauty of the star-studded sky, he asked,

"Would you marry me?"

"Yes," answered the girl softly.

For a very long time the young man is silent. The silence became so oppressive that the girl finally broke it and said:

"Why don't you say something?"

"Hasn't there been said enough for one night?"

*

"Dear Inger," the young Swede called over the phone, "you'll have to forgive me for being so forgetful. I proposed to you last night but really forgot whether you said yes or no."

"Oh, that is all right," answered Inger. "I am glad you called. I knew I said no to somebody last night, but I had entirely forgotten who it was."

*

A new Swedish maid joined the American household. She enquired about her mistress' family.

"I have a son in Yale," says the lady of the house. "I miss him terribly."

"Oh, don't worry. He will get out of it soon. I have a brother who has been in yail already four times."

*

A Finn, a Swede and a Dane were about to be shot by the Gestapo. They were each granted a last wish.

The Finn said, "I would like to drink a last glass of aquavit." The Swede said, "I would like to make a statement." The Dane said, "I would like to be shot before the Swede makes his statement."

*

It is not generally known that God had an assistant when creating the world. About Denmark, that assistant remarked,

"Master, I am afraid you did an injustice to the world; you created a country immune of usual natural disasters. It cannot have avalanches, earthquakes, droughts, floods and volcanic eruptions. Why didn't you give it a fair share of the afflictions which you distributed equitably to other countries?"

"Wait until you have heard the language I gave them!"

*

Why are there no dogs in Iceland?
Because there are no trees!

*

POLAND

At the end of World War II, the USSR and Poland border was being corrected. The new line threatened to run straight through a Polish farm. The Russians proposed to the farmer that they draw a curve around the farm so as to include it in the Soviet territory. The farmer asked for time to reflect and to discuss it with his wife.

The following day he said to the Russians,

"We would prefer that you draw the line on the other side, so that we would remain in Poland."

"Why?" asked the Russians.

"My wife dreads those harsh Russian winters."

*

Easter is coming. The priest and the communist party chief of a Polish village have an argument.

Party chief: "I insist that you reserve the first five rows of the church for the members of the communist party."

Priest: "I will do nothing of the sort."

Party chief: "In that case I will refuse to help carry the canopy on Ascension day."

Priest: "And in that case, I will refuse to write your First of May speech."

*

A Jewish rabbi and a Catholic priest have been fighting with each other all their lives in a small Polish community. When the rabbi is about to die, he calls the priest and asks to be baptized a Catholic. The priest cannot believe his ears but promises to baptize him if he tells the truth why he wanted to be converted. The rabbi promises to reveal his reasons as soon as he has been baptized. Once the rite is completed, he says to the priest: "Now I can die in peace, because after my death the Jewish community will be able to say that there is one Catholic less in the village!"

*

Inspectors visit a farm in Poland and marvel at the size and the weight of the geese. They ask the peasant,

"What do you feed them?"

"They eat any food they can find, but I also give them wheat."

"This is prohibited. Wheat is reserved exclusively for human consumption and we are obliged to fine you."

The peasant warns his neighbour who, when the inspectors come, answers that he never feeds his geese wheat.

"That is a mistake. You would have much better results if you fed them wheat. We are obliged to fine you."

A third farmer who has been warned by his friends, when asked what he fed his geese, answered:

"Nothing."

"What do you mean, nothing?"

"I mean nothing. Every Monday morning I give them one sloty which is the official cost of feeding a goose calculated by the State Planning Commission, and they can go and buy their food where they want!"

*

A Polish teacher is instructed to teach a class on sex. He is in a quandary and says to the children,

"They have asked me to teach you all about love. But I really don't know what to say. I would hate to describe to you love between the same sexes, because it is highly immoral. As for love between different sexes, you know all about it. Therefore, I will talk to you about love between Poland and the Soviet Union."

*

After the election of John Paul II as Pope, his Polish compatriots changed the Ave Maria as follows:

"Hail Mary, full of grace,
For having put the Italians in second place."

*

President Gierik of Poland was invited to the Vatican by Pope John Paul II. The latter suggested to him that he attend Mass. President Gierik accepted and to the great surprise of the Pope he attended the service with utmost fervour and knowledge. When the Mass was over, Pope John Paul said to him,

"You surprised me. I have seldom seen such deep spirituality."

"The truth is that I have a very deep Catholic faith, but I do not practice it."

"And communism?"

"Well, that is just the opposite: I practice it, but I have no faith."

*

A journalist asks a Pole:

"How are your relations with the Soviet Union?"

"Excellent. We send them all our wheat and in return they get all our coal."

*

Question of a teacher to Polish pupils:

"What is the difference between the sun's energy and coal?"

Little Wladek answers: "The sun vanishes in the West and our coal vanishes in the East."

*

A Western journalist asks a Pole about the economic situation in Poland.

"It is average."

"What do you mean by average?"

"It is worse than last year and better than next year."

*

How long does it take to make an omelet in Poland?

Ten minutes to make it and four hours to stand in line to buy the eggs.

*

What does a Polish worker do to show he believes in Communism?

He goes to Mass every day.

*

How many Poles does it take to repair a motorcycle?

None, because there are no parts.

*

One Pole to another:

"Have you heard? A plane carrying the entire Soviet Politburo has crashed in Poland."

"Was anyone saved?"

"Yes. Poland."

*

The Russians have invented a new animal, a crossbreed between a cow and a camel. As a result that animal can graze in Poland and be milked in the Soviet Union!

*

A Polish housewife asks the butcher: "How much is that piece of meat you have in your store?"

"Two hundred slotys."

"How do you know without even weighing it?"

Butcher: "Lady, I weighed this piece of meat already fifty times this morning!"

*

A Pole comes home and finds his wife in the arms of another man. He screams at her: "Is that how you behave, when all other women are standing in line at the butcher's store?"

*

People are lined up for blocks in front of a butcher store in Poland. A little fellow says to a taller man standing in front of him,

"Listen, I am going across the street to buy some cigarettes."

"That's fine," says the tall fellow, "but you didn't have to slap me on my back for that."

"I didn't slap your back. I marked you with a cross of chalk to recognize my place."

*

What is a hundred meters long, has a thousand legs and eats bread?

A line of Polish housewives waiting in front of a butcher store.

*

ROMANIA

At a session of the Romanian Parliament, deputy Antonescu raises a question with the government:

"Mr. President, could you tell us where is the good wheat we harvested last summer? Where is our good wine? Where does our petroleum go? Where are the steel tubes we are producing?"

The President answers that a reply will be given at the next meeting of Parliament.

At that meeting, Antonescu repeats his questions and is told that the government needs more time for a reply.

Several months pass and at a subsequent session of Parliament another representative, Comrade Titulescu, asks,

"Mr. President, where is Comrade Antonescu?"

*

Two Romanian gypsies are playing cards. One of them has lost all he had. He offers to play his wife for 400 lei. His partner considers the price too high. He reduces it to 200 lei. The partner refuses to go along and he finally asks him:

"What would you pay for her?"

"Nothing."

"O.K. You can have her."

*

President Brejnev was visiting Romania. He noticed that the population was very cheerful, happy and smiling. He asked the President of Romania why this was so.

"It is because we have a fabulous joke teller who keeps the population happy with his stories."

Brejnev asked whether he could invite the joke-teller to the USSR and the President of Romania agreed.

When the humorist arrived in Moscow he was received by Brejnev who said to him:

"I am glad that you have come to the USSR. But I must tell you that you will find here a different kind of people; socialism in the Soviet Union has reached much higher standards of achievements than in Romania."

The joke teller looked with surprise at Brejnev,

"I thought that *I* was supposed to tell the jokes?"

*

SPAIN

During Franco's regime, it was strictly prohibited to import any pornographic material into Spain. One day, an elderly American lady arriving from New York on an American flight was asked by the customs official if she had any pornographic material.

The old lady looked up at him in utter surprise,

"My dear young man, how could I! I don't even have a pornograph!"

*

A Spaniard returns to Spain after a pilgrimage to the holy city of Lourdes in France. When he crosses the border, the Spanish customs official finds a bottle of white liquid hidden in his luggage and asks what it is.

"It is holy water from Lourdes." The customs official uncorks the bottle, smells it and says,

"That is not water. It is brandy."

"Jesus, Maria, Josef!" exclaims the Spaniard. "A miracle!"

*

About that Spanish toast "Salud, dinero, y amor" a UN diplomat once remarked,

"Salud is when you do not have dinero for amor."

*

During a visit to Spain, President Carter travelled in an armoured car. The Spaniards complained and pointed out that during his visit to Yugoslavia he walked around freely in the streets, kissing children and shaking hands. Carter explained,

"Yes, but here in Spain there are so many communists!"

*

A Madrid business man has sent his beautiful young wife to a hotel on the beach of Benidorm and promises to join her for the weekend. When he arrives, she falls in his arms passionately and they lock themselves up in the room.

"Oh, my darling, what a joy to have you, what heavenly moments we are going to live together. Could you begin by kissing my ears . . ."

At that point a person from the next room shouts through the wall,

"Do I have to hear the same story every day for a full week?"

*

A UN productivity expert is sent to Spain to help the government achieve a greater labour output in the South. As he arrives in Grenada, he sees a gypsy leaning over the railing of a bridge. The man does nothing except watch the fishermen and the water.

The UN expert asks him:

"How many hours a day do you work?"

"Perhaps an hour."

"Well, your government would like productivity to go up, and if you worked two hours instead of one, your productivity would increase by 100 percent."

"Why should I do that?"

"By doing that you would catch up for example with the productivity of the Germans."

"Why?"

"Because they are very rich. For example, most of them are able to spend a month of vacation in Spain each year."

Gipsy: "But I am already doing that all year round!"

*

An American crew was filming a movie in Spain. The producer hired a gipsy fortune teller to predict the weather. She predicted it very well. When she announced good weather, there was good weather, and when she predicted rain, it would rain. The producer was very happy, especially because he paid her very little for the service. But one day, her predictions became all wrong. The producer asked her what happened. She answered: "My radio broke down."

*

A delegate from Spain to the UN who was obnoxious to everyone was nicknamed "a Spain in the neck."

*

SWITZERLAND

A Swiss schoolteacher asks little Toni:
"Who was the first man on Earth?"
Little Toni: "William Tell."
Schoolteacher: "No, the first man on Earth was Adam."
Little Toni: "Oh, if you include foreigners, of course!"

*

An Italian worker applies for a job with a Swiss construction firm.
Foreman: "What is your name?"
"Enrico Caruso."
"That sounds familiar."
"Yes, I am very well known. I have been working on many building sites in Switzerland."

*

A young man arrived every day on his bicycle at the border between France and Switzerland. On his back he carried a rucksack of sand. The Swiss customs officials made him empty the sack each time to see if anything was hidden in it, but they never could find anything. Still they were convinced that the young man was smuggling something. So one day they said to him,
"Look, young man, we have been trying to figure out what you are smuggling and our best experts cannot find the answer. We are therefore offering you a deal: if you tell us what you smuggle, we promise that we will not prosecute you. You will be free. But for God's sake, tell us what you are smuggling."
The young man looked at them very surprised and said:
"Bicycles!"

*

Swiss schoolboy: "There are five parts of the world: Europe, Asia, Africa, America and Switzerland."

*

A train in Switzerland stops between two stations.

Passenger to conductor: "What is the trouble this time?"

Conductor: "There is a cow on the tracks."

A little while later, the train halts again.

"And what is it now?"

Conductor: "It is a cow on the track."

"What! Another cow?"

Conductor: "No, the same cow!"

*

When the Americans landed on the moon, they were surprised to find a little Chinese flag stuck in the ground. They radioed back this news to the President of the US who sent his representative in Peking to see Mao Tse Tung and ask him if indeed the Chinese had landed on the moon before the Americans. Mae Tse Tung confirmed it.

"But how did you do it?" asked the American.

"Oh, it was simple. As you know, we are so numerous. We just put one Chinese on top of the other until we reached the moon."

But the US astronauts were even more surprised when a little later they found a Swiss flag on the moon. Again they cabled back their discovery to the President of the US who sent his Ambassador to see the President of the Swiss Confederation.

"Is it true that you sent a man on the moon?"

"Yes."

"How on Earth did you do it?"

"It was simple. We took a Spanish worker, put an Italian on top of him, another Spaniard on top of the Italian, and so forth until we reached the moon."

*

Two elderly Swiss ladies are travelling by train from the suburbs of Geneva to the city to do their shopping. One asks the other,

"Did you hear of the World Hunger Campaign launched by the United Nations? Did you contribute to it?"

"Yes, I did. But where exactly is that third world located?"

*

All people descend from Adam and Eve, except the Swiss.

Why?

Because if Adam had been Swiss, instead of eating the apple offered by Eve, he would have made cider to sell.

*

God one day came down on Earth and landed in a meadow in the Swiss Alps where a young maiden was shepherding a herd of cows. God asked her if he could taste a glass of fresh milk and the girl served him one. God thanked her and asked if she was happy or in need of anything.

"Are you satisfied with creation or do you want something?"

"I don't want anything."

"Wouldn't you like to live in the big city?"

"No."

"Wouldn't you like to have a big car?"

"No."

"Wouldn't you like to travel around the world?"

"No."

"That is strange. Isn't there anything which you would want?"

"Yes, there is something."

"What is it. Please tell me."

"I would like you to pay for the glass of milk."

*

A church was hit by lightening and burned down in Switzerland. The priest organized a special collection for the reconstruction of the church. A Swiss peasant refused, on the grounds that he would not give anything to a boss who destroys his own house!

*

In a train which was crossing the Brenner pass from Italy to Switzerland, a young woman was very nervous when the customs control was approaching. A Capuchin monk who was travelling in the same compartment asked her what was the matter.

"I bought a lot of women's underwear in Italy."

The monk replied "Don't worry. Give it to me. I will hide it in my hood."

When the Swiss customs official asked the Capuchin if he had anything to declare, he answered,

"Yes, women's underwear."

"Otherwise you feel all right, Brother?"

*

In England everything is permitted, except what is specifically prohibited.

In Russia everything is prohibited, except what is specifically permitted.

In France everything is permitted, even what is specifically prohibited.

In Switzerland everything is prohibited, even what is specifically authorized.

*

A Swiss soldier was being trained in parachute jumping. The instructor told him

"You jump, you count to three and then you pull the string that will open your parachute."

The recruit jumps, the parachute does not open and the man crashes on the ground. An ambulance comes rushing and as the attendants pick him up, they hear him faintly,

"Three!"

*

Another Swiss parachute candidate goes to a store and buys himself a chute. The salesman explains to him its functioning,

"You pull this first string and the parachute will open."

"And if it does not open?"

"Then you pull this second safety string."

"And if it still does not open?"

"Then you have this third safety string."

"And if that does not open it?"

"Well, then you bring us back the parachute and we will give you another one."

*

At a Swiss railroad station a passenger asks the stationmaster,

"Is there time to take a drink before my train leaves?"

"Yes, especially if you let me have a drink with you."

*

Swiss girl to a shepherd with whom she is sitting in a meadow high up in the Alps,

"Would you like to see where I was operated on for appendicitis?"

"Sure I would."

"Well, it was in that white building down there in the valley."

*

A Swiss couple came out of a supermarket with their merchandise and sat down in the car. The husband stayed at the wheel without making a move. After a while his wife asked,

"Why don't we leave?"

"There is still time left on the parking meter."

*

Why do Swiss peasants have big, heavy cars?

So that they can drive to Bern and complain to the authorities.

*

On top of the list of complaints by Swiss citizens there is this item:

"Delays in the delivery of the latest model of Mercedes-Benz."

*

A Swiss woman asked for a divorce after a year of marriage, complaining that she was still a virgin.

The judge asked the husband for an explanation.

Swiss husband: "I did not know that she was in such a hurry!"

*

A Swiss was asked to describe a machine gun.

He said: "It is a machine that makes bing. . . bing. . . bing. . ., but much faster."

*

"Did you know that William Tell had two sons?"

"No. I thought he had only one."

"The first died during the exercises."

*

Swiss to another Swiss:

"I have a brother who emigrated to the United States."

"How does he like it?"

"I don't know?"

"Doesn't he write to you?"

"Yes, he wrote me a letter, but written on it was: "Return after five days," so I returned it to him."

*

A Swiss train crosses a tunnel. After a while, a foreign passenger comments,

"I have never seen such a long tunnel."

"It is because we are sitting in the last car."

*

Waiter to customer:

"Our cheese is imported from Switzerland."

Gourmet: "Don't you mean "deported" from Switzerland?"

*

A UN diplomat was eating in a Swiss restaurant in New York. He said to the owner:

"You know, your cheese fondue is much better than what they serve in Switzerland."

"Of course," said the manager, "over there they use domestic cheese. Here we use imported cheese."

*

"How do you like Switzerland," a journalist asks a visitor who has just returned from that country.

"Well, if you take away the mountains there is not much left."

*

Why do Swiss cows wear bells?

Because their horns do not work.

*

Shortly after the inclusion by Mr. Mitterand of four Communist Ministers in the French government, this joke was heard in Switzerland.

First Swiss to second Swiss:

"Where will you spend your vacations this year?"

"I have applied for a visa to an Eastern Socialist Country."

★

"Why did you do that? After our hard winter and rainy spring you should go on vacation to a sunny, warm country."

"But I am; I want to go to the French Cote d'Azur."

★

A Swiss talks to his friend:

"I am tired of my wife, but I do not know how to get rid of her."

Friend: "I have a foolproof advice for you: make love to her three times a day and after three weeks she will die."

Three weeks later the friend visits the man at his home. He is lying on a couch on the porch, looks haggard, smokes one cigarette after the other and drinks heavily.

"What is the matter with you? You look awful."

"Well, imagine the situation: look out there and you will see my wife singing and whistling while she is hanging her clothes to dry. And she does not have the faintest idea that by tomorrow she will be dead!"

★

A Swiss taxicab was coming down a steep hill when suddenly the brakes failed and the cab rushed towards disaster. The passenger screamed to the driver,

"Stop the meter, will you!"

★

A Swiss was imprisoned in an asylum because he had deposited money in a foreign country.

★

At the beginning of a schoolyear in a Swiss school, the teacher makes acquaintance with the new children who have arrived all nicely and neatly dressed. To get an idea of the level of their knowledge she asks them a few questions.

The first question is: "Who invented the gear?"

None of the Swiss children knows the answer, but at the rear of the class there is an Italian boy who lifts his hand and who answers:

"Leonardo da Vinci."

The teacher objects: "No, the gear was invented in 1453 by Bernard Schmidt of Zurich."

Her next question is: "Who invented yodling?"

None of the Swiss children knows the answer, but the Italian boy again raises his hand and gives his answer:

"Bernard Schmidt from Zurich."

"What?", exclaims the teacher. "And what makes you believe that?"

Italian Boy: "He invented it when he caught his hand in the gear he had fabricated."

*

UNION OF SOVIET SOCIALIST REPUBLICS

Stalin one day became very annoyed with the incessant jokes against him from an Armenian radio commentator. He called the man,

"How can you tell such ugly jokes about me? It is intolerable. I am doing all I can for my country. I have raised the standard of living by at least fifty per cent. I have obtained respect for the Soviet Union in the world. I have brought science and technology to unprecedented heights. I have. . ." and on he went. On the other end of the line, the Armenian commentator remained silent, until Stalin shouted,

"Well, what do you have to say?"

"I was listening carefully. I have not told any of these jokes."

*

During one of his speeches Stalin declared,

"I am ready to give my blood, drop by drop, for the Soviet people."

And a voice from the audience countered: "Why don't you give it all at once?"

*

Stalin announced to the Soviet people that on the way to communism every family would soon receive a new apartment, a new car and finally an airplane.

"Why an airplane?" asked someone.

"So that you can fly to Georgia and buy potatoes when there are none in Moscow," answered someone else.

*

An elderly woman ran to catch a bus and as she sat down, she exclaimed, "Thank God."

Her neighbour remarked, "This is an atheistic country. You must say, Thank Stalin."

"And what will I say when Stalin is dead?"

"Then you can say Thank God."

*

During a Moscow Mayday parade, a man carried a poster which said "Thank you, Komrad Stalin, for my happy childhood."

NKVD officers approached the man to ask why.

"You are too old. Stalin was not even born when you were a child."

"That is exactly what I am thanking him for."

*

Stalin has lost his preferred pipe. He complains to Beria, the chief of the secret police. The following morning Beria reports to him that 500 people have been arrested, but that the pipe could not be found.

A day later Stalin finds his pipe and tells Beria the

good news. Beria comments grimly,

"That is too bad, because already 400 suspects have confessed."

*

Three inmates are talking in a concentration camp at the height of the Stalin purges. The first says

"I was arrested for opposing Bukharin." The second says,

"I was arrested for backing Bukharin." The third says,

"I am Bukharin."

*

Stalin's mother visits him for the first time in Moscow. She is a very elderly lady who has lived all her life in a tiny Georgian village. Her son proudly shows her his luxurious offices and private apartments in the capital. Then he takes her to his superb datcha in the woods, equipped with all the latest conveniences. Finally, they fly on his private plane to his villa on the Black Sea and he asks her,

"Little mother, what do you think? Aren't you proud of your son?"

"I am overwhelmed. But aren't you afraid that the Reds will take all this away from you?"

*

People are lined up for blocks in front of a butcher shop in Moscow. They have been waiting since seven o'clock and at ten the store is not yet open. A fellow becomes very upset and says to his neighbour,

"I am going to the Kremlin to punch Khrushchev in the nose. I am sick and tired of this situation." He leaves, but after a while he comes back and resumes his place in the line.

The other fellow says,

"What happened? Did you tell Khrushchev how you felt?"

"No.The line of people to punch Khruschchev in the nose is much longer than this one."

★

When Khrushchev visited the airport of London, he asked how many people they employed.

"2000."

"That is a lot. In the Soviet Union we would run such an airport with half that number."

"Yes, but we have so many communists."

★

One morning at the Teheran conference, Roosevelt was talking to Churchill.

"I dreamt last night that I was president of the world."

Churchill replied, "And I dreamt that I was the world's prime minister."

At that point, Stalin, who had just entered the conference room overhearing them, commented,

"I don't remember having appointed either of you."

★

Stalin dies and arrives in heaven and St. Peter tells him,

"For a man like you, there is no choice. You will go to hell."

He opens a door and shows him a scene of damned people lying on beds of upright nails and being flogged by devils equipped with leaden whips.

"All I can offer you," says St. Peter, "is a choice between capitalist hell and communist hell."

"I will take communist hell," says Stalin. "I am sure there they don't have any nails."

★

The Czar of Russia and Stalin meet in the afterworld. They compare living conditions during their respective periods. The Czar holds the view that everything was better in his time, and Stalin thinks the opposite. When they come to the subject of liquors, the Czar asks,

"How strong is your vodka nowadays? Ours was 30 percent proof."

"Communist vodka is much stronger. It is 40 percent proof."

The Czar ponders for a while and then concludes,

"Well, I think it was not worthwhile to make a revolution over 10 percent!"

*

An aide of Kosygin reports to him at the Kremlin:

"Comrade First Secretary, there are two thousand soldiers eating luncheon on Red Square."

"That's fine. It is a nice, sunny spring day. I am so glad that they are enjoying themselves."

An hour later, the same aide returns and reports to Kosygin that there are now five thousand soldiers having luncheon on Red Square.

"That's wonderful. But why do you look so worried."

"Because they all eat with chop-sticks!"

*

One morning President Brezhnev arrives very early at his office in the Kremlin and as he looks out of the window, he see the sunrise above the horizon. He looks romantically at the star which suddenly speaks to him,

"Good morning, Mr. Brezhnev."

"Good morning, sun. How nice it is of you to greet me."

At noontime he remembers the early morning scene and he goes to the window to look up at the sun. The sun greets him again warmly:

"Good day, Mr. Brezhnev," and he is very pleased.

In the evening, Brezhnev goes to a window on the opposite side of his office to see the sunset. The sun is about to begin its descent behind the horizon and it remains totally silent. Brezhnev asks,

"Dear sun, you were so nice this morning and at noon. Why don't you talk to me anymore?"

The sun, with a dark, unfriendly voice answers, "I don't have to any more. Now I am in the West."

*

President Nixon was visiting Moscow. At breakfast, Brezhnev and he were telling each other about the dreams they had during the night.

Brezhnev: "I dreamt that I was standing in front of the Capitol in Washington and I saw a familiar flag flying on top of it — a red flag with the hammer and sickle."

Nixon: "I dreamt that I was standing on Red Square and I saw the Kremlin all covered with huge inscriptions."

Brezhnev: "What did they say?"

Nixon: "I could not tell. There were all in Chinese."

*

Brezhnev one day wanted to know what the people really thought of him. He went incognito to a bar and asked a man at the counter how he felt about Brezhnev.

The man answered, "Shh! Let us go outside and I will tell you."

Outdoors Brezhnev repeated his question, but the man asked him to be quiet and to go along with him to Red Square.

There Brezhnev repeated his question and the man said,

"Shh. Let us go to the middle of Red Square where nobody can hear us."

In the middle of Red Square, after making sure that no one could listen, the man whispered into the ear of Brezhnev,

"I like Brezhnev!"

*

Brezhnev holds a meeting with all his ministers and says:

"Comrades, I have good news for you. Before the year is over, the entire world will be communist."

The Minister of Agriculture looks quite worried and asks,

"Where will we then get the wheat from?"

*

President Brezhnev visits President Carter in Washington. At one point, President Carter wishes to consult President Roosevelt and he asks his Secretary if it is possible to place a telephone call to hell. After enquiry she says:

"Yes, but it is very expensive. It would cost you 1000 dollars a minute."

In view of the high price, President Carter gives up his thought.

A few weeks later, President Brezhnev, back in Moscow wishes to consult Stalin and he puts the same question to his Secretary. After a while she comes back and says:

"You can call hell without any difficulty."

"How much does it cost?"

"Ten cents."

"How is that possible? In Washington it costs 1000 dollars."

"Yes, but here it is a local call."

*

At the time of the labour unrest and martial law in Poland, President Brezhnev went to a barbershop in Moscow. The barber asked him, "How is the situation in Poland, Comrad President?"

Brezhnev was furious and asked him to mind his own business. A little while later when the barber repeated his question he got the same answer. When the barber asked the same question for the third time, Brezhnev blew up and asked,

"Why on earth are you so concerned with what is going on in Poland?"

"I am not concerned at all, but everytime I ask you the question, your hair stands straight up and it is easier for me to cut it."

*

The President of the Soviet Union visits the United States. The President of the United States shows him the latest American computer.

"This computer can predict the future of any country. For example, here is a print-out of the future of the United States during the next fifty years."

The Russian President examines the material and asks,

"Could you ask the machine to give me its views about the future of the Soviet Union?"

"Be my guest," and the President of the U.S. presses the necessary buttons.

After a while he hands a batch of papers to his Russian colleague.

The latter examines the print-outs.

"What does it say?"

"I don't know. I cannot read anything. It is all written in Chinese."

*

A Russian leader and his wife return from Paris to Moscow by train. During the night, she asks him what country they are in. At the next station, he lets his hand hang out of the window and then withdraws it.

"We are in East Germany."

"How do you know?"

"Someone kissed my hand."

Sometime later, the wife asks the same question and he hangs his hand out again.

"We are now in Poland."

"How do you know?"

"Because someone bit my hand."

The same scene reoccurs later during the night and he reports that they are now in the Soviet Union.

"How do you know?"

"Someone stole my watch."

*

A Russian couple in Moscow had a parrot who liked to repeat "Down with communism." The couple was denounced by their neighbours and one evening the police arrived. Quickly they hid the parrot in the freezer. The police searched the entire apartment and could not find anything. Just before leaving it occurred to one of the men to look into the freezer where he found the frozen bird.

After having thawed, the parrot started to shout,

"Hail Brezhnev; hail communism." The policemen were delighted and left happily.

The couple asked the parrot,

"Why did you change your mind and suddenly praise communism?"

"Look, anyone who has just returned from Siberia like me would do the same!"

*

"Ah, Moscow is an astonishing city!" exclaimed Brigitte Bardot, returning to Paris from a trip to the Soviet Union. "I was walking all naked in the streets, wearing only shoes, and everybody was looking at my feet!"

*

A high UN official visits the Soviet Union for the first time. He is taken on a sightseeing tour which includes the Moscow zoo. There he is astonished to see a wolf and a lamb living peacefully in the same cage.

"How extraordinary! How do you manage to have a wolf and a lamb live so happily together? This is real peaceful coexistence!"

"It is very simple. Everyday we put in a new lamb."

*

What is the difference between English fairy tales and Russian fairy tales?

English tales begin with the words: "Once upon a time." Russian tales start with: "Once in the future."

*

Teacher: "How many crops does the Soviet Union have?"

Pupil: "Four: one in Poland, one in Hungary, one in Romania and one in the Soviet Union.

*

The devil was pursuing a car occupied by President Brezhnev, President Nixon and the Premier of Hungary. Nixon tried to shoot the devil, but to no avail. Brezhnev tried to stop him with a bazooka but he was no more effective. Then the Premier of Hungary took a piece of paper, wrote something on it and threw it to the devil who disappeared instantly.

Brezhnev and Nixon asked

"What did you write on that note which was so effective?"

"I wrote that we were on the road to perfect communism."

*

A woman keeps calling Brezhnev, asking him for his intervention to get her first a car, then a mink-coat and finally a dacha. With each request she says:

"Do you remember how we slept together?" Brezhnev finally asks, "Could you remind me when exactly I slept with you?"

"You don't remember? It was during the speech of Komrad Suslov during the thirtieth Congress of the Central Party Committee."

*

The schoolchildren of a school in the Soviet Union were asked to give the definition of socialism. One child answered,

"It is a system in which all the means of reproduction belong to the State."

*

On election day in the Soviet Union the citizens are lined up in front of city hall and are given sealed envelopes to drop into the ballot box. One peasant tears the envelope open, whereuponhthe police surrounds him and shouts,

"Comrade! What are you doing? Don't you know that this is a secret ballot?"

*

A plane flying to Moscow was seized by Arabs and detoured towards Cairo. One of the passengers, a Georgian, managed to disarm the hijacker and to put the plane back on its course.

When they arrived in Moscow he received a hero's welcome. He was asked what had prompted him to such a courageous act. He answered,

"I was bringing 500 kilos of oranges to Moscow for sale on the black market. I could not have sold them in Cairo."

*

A Russian went to the police to ask for permission to emigrate to the US.

"Aren't you happy here?" asked the police.

"I have no complaints."

"Are you dissatisfied with your job?"

"I have no complaints."

"Then why do you want to go to America?"

"Because there I can have complaints."

*

President X, a communist economist, was running his country so hard that all resources and goods disappeared. The Russians decided to send him as an expert to the Sahara where he could do no harm. After a few weeks, he sent a cable to Moscow: "Please send sand. There is no sand left in the Sahara."

*

A Russian schoolteacher asks his pupils:

"How tall was Lenin?"

A boy answers immediately: "Five feet and three inches."

"How do you know?"

"Because my father is six feet two inches and every day he holds his hand up to his neck and says I have had Lenin up to here."

*

A communist worker returns home after an evening of political indoctrination. He says pensively to his wife,

"There are quite a few things I didn't understand. For example, our party leader said that communism was on the horizon. What did he mean by that?"

"Why don't you look it up in the dictionary?"

He does so and then exclaims,

"Now I understand. He was perfectly right. Horizon means an imaginary line which recedes as you try to get closer to it."

*

A communist village board meets to consider the following agenda:

1. the construction of a new road
2. the building of a new barn
3. the building of communism

An elder comments:

"Comrades, you know perfectly well that we don't have any funds to build a new road and we don't have wood to build a new barn. Consequently I move that we pass straight to item 3 on our agenda."

*

A Russian arrives in hell. Satan asks him if he wants to go to capitalist hell or communist hell.

Russian: "To communist hell."

Satan: "You are all the same, you Bolsheviks."

Russian: "It has nothing to do with Bolshevism. The reason is that in communist hell they are using Russian oil which burns much less than capitalist oil."

*

A long queue of people is standing in front of a butcher shop in Moscow.

When the shop opens, the butcher comes out and

invites all those who are members of the communist party to step in the store. The people are furious. When the party members come out, one of the ladies in the line gives vent to her outrage and draws this answer from a party member:

"Comrad, is it not normal that we party members should be the first to be informed that there is no meat?"

*

Russian proverb:

If you have a good head on your shoulders you will always find a chair for your behind.

*

A high Soviet official comes home after work to take his wife to a performance at the Bolshoi opera. He finds her crying and shouting at him, for she has just found out that he has a mistress. He tries to calm her and insists that she accompany him to the Opera where his absence would be noticed. She is still crying when they sit down in their reserved seats. He explains to her calmly,

"You see, my dear, it is very difficult for me to act differently from my superiors. They all have mistresses. For example, my minister has a mistress and she is here tonight." And he points at a woman sitting in a loge. He says the same thing about the vice-minister and his head of department and points each time at their mistresses who are present at the Opera. Whereupon his wife asks if his mistress is also present.

"Yes," and he points at a gorgeous young female.

Whereupon the wife dries up her tears, smiles and says to him,

"Ivan Ivanovich, I am very proud of you. Our mistress is the most beautiful!"

*

An American businessman visits Kiev in the company of a guide. Whenever the guide points at a building, the American asks:

"How long did it take to build?"

"Two years, or perhaps three."

"Well, in the United States it would have taken us barely six months."

After this has happened several times, the Ukranian guide becomes rather nervous, and when they see the new building of the University and the American asks how long it took to build it, he answers:

"I don't have the faintest idea. This building was not here last week."

*

An American and a Russian are talking about their ways of travelling.

American: "I take a Cadillac to go to my office. My wife takes a Vega to do her shopping and when we go to Europe, we rent a Volkswagen."

Russian: "I go to the office by subway. My wife takes the bus for her shopping and when we go to Europe, we use a tank."

*

A journalist called the Armenian radio station and complained that the broadcasts were becoming fainter and fainter.

Armenian radio: "It is because we now broadcast from Siberia."

"And what are you doing there?"

"We are building a bridge. On one side work all those who asked questions. On the other side work those who answered them."

*

Once,in a Russian airplane factory they were trying to build a plane that could fly three times faster than sound (Mach III). Unfortunately, each time a prototype attained that speed, the wings would fall off. The engineers were at a loss and were standing around a new model when they heard a bystander say:

"The solution to your problem is very simple. All you have to do is bore holes along the lines where the wings are attached to the body of the plane."

In desperation, the engineers made this modification and to their immense surprise and joy the plane broke the Mach III sound barrier without losing its wings.

A big celebration was organized to honour the man who had had that luminous idea. The head of the factory praised him to the sky, but when his turn came to say a few words, he simply said:

"You are mistaken. I am not the greatest aerodynamics engineer in the world. I am not even an engineer. I am a toilet cleaner, but in my profession I had observed that no toilet paper ever tears along the perforated lines. I concluded that the same would be true for your plane."

*

On the occasion of the fiftieth anniversary of the October Revolution, Lenin was resuscitated. He received an enthusiastic reception by the Russian people, after which he asked for a hotel room and for a copy of the Pravda. Soon thereafter he was seen dashing out of the hotel and hopping into a taxi.

Cab driver: "Where do you want me to take you?"

Lenin: "To the airport. I am returning to Switzerland to start it all over."

*

Karl Marx came back to Earth and was amazed at the possibilities offered by modern communications. He said to Brezhnev,

"How lucky you are! You can speak directly to hundreds of millions of people through television, whereas during my time I had to write my wits out and to speak interminably to small audiences."

"It is not as easy as you think. As a matter of fact, why don't you try. We offer you this satellite television channel to express your views, but we can give you only very little time. Make it therefore very short, please,"

Karl Marx thought it over and then said only one sentence:

"Workers of the world, please forgive me."

*

When Giorgio La Pira, Mayor of Florence, visited Moscow, he was challenged for his deep Christian beliefs. A communist ideologist asked him,

"How, for example, can you explain the condemnation of the great scientist Galileo by the Church?"

La Pira answered, "Very simple. There were many Stalinists in the Holy See at that time!"

*

Is it possible to make Paris a socialist city?

Yes. But it would be such a shame.

*

A Russian school inspector asks the children to tell him who were the first communists.

Little boy: "Adam and Eve."

Inspector: "Why?"

Little boy: "Because they were naked, everything was prohibited and yet they were told they lived in Paradise."

*

An American Senator visits Moscow. He is shown the highpoints of Soviet achievements among which are the famous, beautiful Moscow subways. His guide says to him proudly,

"Every three minutes you will see a train stop at this platform to take on and discharge passengers."

The American wants to see that. They wait for three minutes, five minutes, ten minutes, a quarter of an hour, and no train arrives.

The American expresses his surprise, whereupon the Soviet guide snaps back,

"Yes, but how about your racial discrimination in the United States?"

*

An American correspondent put this question to a Soviet computer: "How long will it take until perfect communism is achieved?"

Computer: "1500 kilometers."

"What does that mean?" asks the American.

"Well, the machine has been programmed with the information that during each Five Year Plan communism will make a step ahead."

*

A few years ago a foreign visitor expressed surprise to see so many rats and mice in the Kremlin.

"We had to kill all the cats."

"Why?"

"Because they were roaming all over, repeating: Mao, Mao . . ."

*

A Russian airplane carrying two thousand orchids was being hi-jacked to Paris. The pilot convinced the hi-jacker to give up his plan by saying,

"What will you do with 2000 orchids in Paris? Unlike Moscow, you will find no black market for them in Paris."

*

An American couple was visiting Moscow and took lodging in one of the old, fashionable, big hotels from the time of the Czars. Before going to sleep, the husband said:

"I am sure this room is bugged." He searched every place where there could be a listening device. Finally he unrolled the carpet and found a round copper plate affixed on the floor.

"I found it," he exclaimed and with a knife he unscrewed the plate and removed it.

The following morning, as the couple passed by the front desk, the manager of the hotel asked:

"How did you sleep?"

"Very well, thank you."

"I am glad to hear that, because in the room below yours there was a big accident: the old, heavy, crystal chandelier fell from the ceiling and nearly killed the guests in that room."

*

UNITED KINGDOM

Two Frenchmen visit England for the first time. In the streets of London they see with astonishment a group of Scots wearing kilts. One Frenchman asks the other,

"Of what sex can these people be? They look like men, but are dressed like women!"

Second Frenchman: "They are from Middlesex!"

*

An English schoolmaster asks a pupil,

"Where was Nelson killed?"

"In Trafalgar Square."

"Well, then I suppose that Wellington was killed at Waterloo Station?"

"No, that was Napoleon."

*

During the war a Russian spy is parachuted over Wales. He lands in a field near where he is to contact a Welsh spy. On the outskirts of the village he meets a man whom he asks for the whereabouts of a Mr. Jones. The man asks astonished: "Which Jones are you looking for? We have many Jones' in the village; there is Jones the miller, Jones the baker, Jones the butcher. As a matter of fact, I myself am a Jones!"

The spy's face lights up. This might be his contact.

He therefore pronounces the password,
"The sun rises in the East."
The peasant exclaims:
"Oh! You want to see Jones the Spy!"

*

U.S. soldiers stationed in Great Britain during the second world war used to say that the British were overpolite, overcautious and overwitty.

The British retaliated by saying that the Americans were overfed, oversexed and overhere!

*

Britisher to Scotsman:

"How is it that you Scots are so intelligent? You occupy some of the highest positions in England. The President of the British Railroads is a Scot, the Chairman of the National Coal Board is a Scot, and so forth and so on. . ."

"It is because we eat plenty of Scottish fish."

"Is that so? Would you perhaps be so kind and bring me some each week when you return from Scotland?"

"With pleasure." And the Scot regularly brings the Englishman Scottish fish every Monday morning.

After a month, the Englishman complains:

"I do not notice the slightest improvement."

"You must have patience. It takes time."

Another month passes. The Englishman complains again:

"I still don't see any change. By the way, aren't you charging me too much for your fish? Your price is twice that of the market."

Scotsman: "You see, it is beginning to work!"

*

Attlee to Churchill:

"I am going to fire my driver. He nearly got me killed."

Churchill: "Give him another chance."

*

An Englishman and an American argue about the pronunciation of the word schedule. The American maintains that it is pronounced: skedule. The Englishman argues that one says shedule and he lines up a whole series of arguments in his favour.

The American finally gives up and exclaims:

"OK, skit, have it your way."

*

A persistent question in the UK is whether males can be rendered pregnant.

The answer is no, but they keep trying!

*

A drunken Scot is walking home from a party in a neighbouring village. A friend had given him a bottle of home-made Scotch. As he walks on the main road a car passes very close to him and he falls into a ditch along the road. He feels a liquid running along his leg, tastes it with his finger and exclaims:

"Thank God! It is only blood!"

*

Two English males are the only survivors from a sunken passenger boat. They are stranded together on the same deserted island. After a week, one of them finally decides to speak to the other:

"British?"

"Yes. And you?"

"British too."

After another week he has a second question:

"Homosexual?"

"Yes. And you?"

"Me too."

After a third week he asks this question:

"Oxford?"

"No. Cambridge."

"Too bad."

*

An English girl is getting married and her mother advises:

"It is quite possible that it will be a very painful and unpleasant experience. If it should be so, close your eyes and think of England."

*

An Englishman was sitting quietly in his club, when a friend came up to him and said,

"Sorry to hear that you buried your wife yesterday."

The old Englishman answered,

"Had to. She was dead, you know."

*

Why does the sun never set on the British Empire?

Because God would never trust the English in the dark.

*

An Italian worker who worked in Scotland needed an urgent blood transfusion. The hospital did not have any. One of the Scottish workers, attracted by the offer of a good price, gave the necessary blood and the Italian paid him ten pounds for it.

A few days later the Italian needed another blood transfusion, but he offered only half the price to his Scottish friend. The latter accepted, because it was still good money.

A week later the Italian needed a third blood transfusion and he asked his Scottish friend to help him out again. The Scotsman accepted, but after the transfusion he waited in vain for any money. He said to the Italian,

"Why don't you at least pay me the cut-rate price you paid me last time?"

The Italian answered,

"I cannot, because now my blood is entirely Scottish!"

*

An Englishman arrives by boat in Cairo. Arabs surround him and say:

"I have a beautiful girl for you. Only 50 pounds."

Another Arab offers him a woman for 30 pounds. A third one has an offer for 25 pounds.

The Britisher exclaims: "I want to see the British Consul."

Arabs: "Oh, that will be much more expensive!"

*

Two Britishers in a club:

"Don't you think that these lonely meals at the club induce many members to seek marriage?"

"Not as many as marriage induces to come to the club."

*

YUGOSLAVIA

During one of the non-aligned conferences in Yugoslavia, numerous black African delegates could be seen in the streets of Belgrade. A Yugoslav commented to another,

"Don't you think that our gypsies are getting awfully dark these days?"

*

A Yugoslav goes to church one Saturday afternoon and sees a large crowd in it. He asks a bystander:

"What is going on? Why is the church so crowded?"

"A gypsy is confessing his sins."

*

How do gypsy recipes start?

"You steal a dozen eggs . . ."

*

A gipsy with his bear arrives late one evening at an inn. There are no rooms left and the two are lodged in the hayloft. When the gipsy has his supper at the inn, the maid asks if as usual she can spend the night with him. He declines this time, because he is very tired. During the night, however, the maid cannot resist and she goes to the barn.

The following morning, at breakfast, the maid asked the gipsy:

"Did you rest well?"

"Yes. Wonderfully. How about you? But what on earth has happened to you? You look terrible. I have never seen you with such deep blue circles around your eyes!"

"Well, I came to the barn, but I didn't have the heart to wake you up. You slept so well. So I made love with your friend, the fellow with the fur-coat, and, dear God, what a night he had in store for me!"

*

A Yugoslav worker takes a political test.

Interrogator: "What was the political regime of our country before World War II?"

Worker: "It was capitalism."

"And what was capitalism?"

"The exploitation of the workers by the rich."

"Good. And what preceded capitalism?"

"Monarchy, the exploitation of the people by kings and noblemen."

"And before monarchy?"

"Feudalism, the exploitation of the people by the landlords."

"Good. Now let us turn to the future. After socialism, what will be next?"

"Communism, under which everybody will be equal and will receive according to his needs."

"Excellent. And what will there be after communism?"

"Well, I think there will be no other way but to return to the pre-war situation."

*

A gipsy went to the office of the Communist party to register as a member of the party. He was told that he would have to reform his living habits in order to merit being a member of the party. He was asked:

"Would you be ready to give up smoking?"

He was unpleasantly surprised, but finally agreed with some reluctance.

"Would you be ready to give up fooling around with other women and be faithful to your wife?"

Again he seemed shocked but after a while he agreed.

"Finally, would you be ready to give your life for the party?"

"O yes, I don't see any difficulty in that, because life will not be worth living anymore."

*

Two gypsies walk together when it suddenly begins to rain. One of them has an umbrella. He opens it but his friend notices that it is full of holes.

"Why did you take along an umbrella full of holes?"

"I didn't think it would rain."

*

A Montenegran is walking with an ox on a country road in Yugoslavia. A Macedonian comes from the other direction. When they meet, the Macedonian asks,

"Where are you taking this donkey?"

"It is not a donkey; it is an ox."

"I was not talking to you. I was talking to the ox."

*

A famous joke teller has been in prison for quite some time for telling jokes against President Tito. One day, Tito has him brought to his office and says,

"I will have you released if for once you tell a joke in which I am not involved."

"I have one: your wife is pregnant!"

*

The Secretary General of the UN arrives in heaven where he sees the strangest couples: President Kekkonen married to Mrs. Golda Meier and President Tito with Brigitte Bardot. He complains to St. Peter:

"Is that how you recompense earthly behaviour?"

"You've got it all wrong. Brigitte Bardot is not a recompense for President Tito: *he* is the punishment for Brigitte Bardot."

*

A Yugoslav is discussing politics with an Albanian. He says,

"What pretensions can you have? You are such a tiny, insignificant country."

"Quite the contrary. Together with the Chinese we are more than 1 billion people!"

*

An American once asked a Yugoslav,

"What will happen if President Tito dies?"

Yugoslav: "And what will happen to you if President Reagan reaches 87?"

*

A Montenegran was visiting a Serbian friend. The Serbian asked him to help him change an electric bulb in the ceiling. The Montenegran climbed on the shoulders of his friend. After a while the Serbian asked him,

"Are you finished?"

"No. I am waiting."

"What are you waiting for?"

"I am waiting for you to turn."

*

A Yugoslav is riding on a horse, with his wife in much pain walking behind him.

A friend passing by asks the man,

"Where are you going?"

"I am taking her to the hospital."

NORTH AMERICA

CANADA

A French Canadian UN delegate has fallen into the East River. He calls for help,

"Au secours, au secours!" An English Canadian who passes by hears him and shouts,

"If instead of learning French you had learned how to swim, you would not be in this ordeal!"

*

A Canadian widower has a terrible nightmare each night. He sees his demised wife bathing in a pond of fire in hell. The flames reach up to her chin. She suffers terribly. He talks to his priest about the dream. The latter advises him that much prayer and special masses are needed, as well as donations for good causes. The widower therefore gives to the priest a substantial sum of money.

The following week the priest asks him if his dreams are still the same.

"No. The situation has substantially improved. The flames have diminished and reach only up to her waist. But she still suffers a lot."

"Well, more money is needed for prayers, masses and charitable causes." The widower hands another sum to the priest.

And the same happens week after week until one day the flames reach only the ankles of the deceased woman. The priest suggests further donations, but the widower argues,

"I think we better leave it at that, because my poor wife always had awfully cold feet."

*

A Canadian Bishop inspects a village parish where he has to stay overnight. The priest lives all alone in the parish house and has no other bed to offer but his own. The Bishop agrees to share it with him. The following morning, when the cock crows, the half-awaken Bishop taps the shoulder of the priest who hears him say,

"Marie, please get up and prepare breakfast."

*

A Canadian Bishop inspects a village parish where he notices that the priest lives with two pretty young female maids.

"How come you break the church law according to which a priest's servant must have reached the age of 40?"

"Well, I could not find a forty year old woman, so I decided to take two twenty year old girls."

*

A Canadian Catholic girl is going out with a young man. They are deeply in love and one day she announces to her parents that they intend to get married. Alas, the young man is a Protestant and the parents refuse their authorization. They suggest that she try to convert him to Catholicism. A few weeks later, one evening, the girl comes home crying.

"What is the matter?" asks her mother.

"I have talked so much to him about Catholicism that he has decided to become a priest!"

*

A Canadian went to confession. He told the priest that he had sinned with a woman. The priest asked him who the woman was, but the Canadian refused to say.

"Was it Mrs. So and So from Champlain Alley?"

"No."

"Was it Mrs. So and So from St. Marie street?"

"No."

"Was it the young blonde wife of Mr. So and So from Cathedral Lane?"

"No."

The priest gave up and when the Canadian left the confessional he rubbed his hands with pleasure, saying: "I got three new addresses!"

*

A shoemaker to a Canadian polar explorer:

"Here are your new boots for your next expedition. How did you like the last ones?"

"They were delicious."

*

UNITED STATES

A New Yorker who was tired of being robbed, left this note affixed at the door of his apartment when he went out shopping:

"I may not hear the bell. I am far back in the kitchen."

When he returned he found his place ransacked again. The robber had left a note on the kitchen table:

"I looked for you everywhere, but I could not find you."

*

In a New York movie house, a woman's voice suddenly can be heard shouting at someone:

"Take your hands off, you!"

And a little later, in a softer tone:

"Not you."

*

One Irish woman to another Irish woman in New York City:

"Mary, how come you stopped having children? For four consecutive years, you had a child, and now suddenly you have stopped completely."

Mary: "Well, I heard that every fifth child in New York is a Jew. So I stopped. I do not want to have a Jewish child in an Irish family."

*

A family of pigeons living in upper Manhattan has invited a pigeon from lower Manhattan for dinner. At seven o'clock the meal is ready but the invited pigeon has not arrived. The hosts wait for him for almost three hours. When he finally arrives, they ask him,

"What took you so long?"

"Oh! It was such a lovely evening that I felt like walking."

*

New York has become such a predominantly Jewish city that the Mother Superiors of the few remaining Catholic convents are being called Mother Shapiro!

*

Two young New Yorkers meet in the street.

"I did not see you for a long time," comments the first to the second. "Where have you been hiding?"

"I got married."

"When?"

"Six weeks ago."

"Can I still congratulate you."

*

A New York woman is talking to her doctor's nurse:

"Miss, could you check the doctor's office and see if you can find my bra. He examined me yesterday and I think I forgot it there."

The nurse makes a thorough search and calls her back:

"I looked everywhere but I could not find it."

"Never mind," answers the lady. "In that case I must have left it at the dentist."

*

A worried New Yorker presents himself at the morgue and asks if by any chance they have the body of his wife:

"She left the house, saying that she would commit suicide."

Attendant: "Let us see. Did she have any particular sign by which she could be recognized?"

"Yes. She stutters."

*

"What is the name of your college?"

"I don't know. I am only on the football team."

*

A New York priest and a rabbi are arguing whether Jesus was more Catholic than Jewish. The rabbi holds firmly the view that Jesus remained a perfect Jew, physically, intellectually and spiritually.

"As a matter of fact, after 2000 years Jews today still look like him. I am a perfect replica of Jesus." The priest looks in utter astonishment at the bearded rabbi, so the latter says,

"Come along with me, I will prove it to you." He takes the priest to a women's house and knocks at the door. The lady of the establishment opens and when she sees the rabbi she exclaims, "Oh, Jesus Christ, not you again!"

*

A new soprano singing for the first time at the Metropolitan Opera in New York gets a reasonable amount of applause after her first major aria and decides to sing an encore. That finished she receives again a moderate applause and decides to sing a third time. At that time someone from the audience encourages her:

"Bravo, Miss. Don't give up. Perhaps the third time you will get it right."

*

After his death, Cardinal Spellman of New York asks to be admitted at the gates of heaven. St. Peter checks the name in his registry under the professional category "religion," but cannot find it. He asks Spellman if by any chance the name could be listed under another profession.

"Try real estate."

Sure enough.

*

Americans like to exaggerate about their great men to such an extent that someone once said,

"Abraham Lincoln was one of our most beloved presidents. He was born in a log cabin which he built with his own hands."

*

Rabbi Isaac Rosenduft is driving behind Reverend Mac Carthy on Riverside Drive in New York. At a red light, the inattentive rabbi bumps into the rear of Father Mac Carthy and causes substantial damage to his car. The rabbi goes to the reverend, apologizes profusely and offers him a gulp of whiskey. After a while, noticing the priest's increasing paleness, the rabbi offers him another generous gulp of scotch. Feeling better Father Mac Carthy says to the rabbi,

"Thank you for your kindness. You do not look well either. You better take a shot of whiskey yourself."

"Oh! No," comments the rabbi. "Aren't we waiting for the police?"

*

A Frenchman visited New York for the first time. At the end of his stay he is asked for his impressions.

"Well, it is a fantastic city, no doubt. It has many astonishing attractions and features, but there is one thing I could not stand, namely the racial discrimination against the Blacks. You would never find such a thing in my country."

"And how did you like your hotel accomodation?"

"Oh, it was all right, except for one thing: all those Puerto-Ricans and Haitians on the staff."

*

A Jew visits Rockefeller at his castle on top of a hill near Tarrytown. He says to him: "I have bought the hill opposite yours and I want to build on it exactly the same castle as yours. Would you allow me to look around and to take measurements."

"Of course," says Rockefeller, "be my guest."

A year later, the Jew's castle is completed and he invites "Rockefeller to visit it."

Rockefeller cannot believe his eyes: it is an absolutely perfect replica of his mansion. The Jew asks him for his opinion:

"It is an extremely accurate copy. I congratulate you."

Jew: "There is however one big difference between my castle and yours."

"I cannot see any."

"I don't have a Jew as a neighbour!"

*

The wife of a vice-president of the United States once asked the Pentagon to send an officer as an escort for her daughter's trip. The mother specified no one Jewish. The following morning a young black officer rang the bell and the lady exclaimed:

"Who on earth sent you?"

"Colonel Cohen, Madam."

*

When Mrs. Golda Meier, the Premier of Israel visited President Nixon, the latter said to her,

"Mrs. Meier, you have such good generals. Just look how deplorable mine are in Viet Nam. Would it not be possible to make an exchange? For one of your good generals, I would offer you two."

"Alright. Which one would you like?"

"May I have General Dayan?"

"Yes."

"And which generals would you like in return?"

"General Motors and General Electric!"

⋆

Definition of an American businessman: someone who wants his government to be the biggest and strongest in the world and intervene for his benefit in the affairs of all nations, but does not want it to intervene in anything at home and in his affairs.

⋆

Complaint of a husband to his friend:

"My wife is *extremely* jealous. When she finds a hair on my clothes she goes absolutely mad. Lately she hasn't found anything, and still she is furious."

"How can that be?"

"She believes I am going out with a bald woman!"

⋆

A young woman saw that her neighbour, whose husband earned the same income as hers, had been able to buy a brand-new mink-coat. How on earth had she done it?

"It was very simple. Each time my husband became romantic I asked him for the modest sum of ten dollars. I put these little offerings aside until I had the sum to buy a mink-coat."

Her friend believes this a wonderful idea and in the evening, when her husband became amorous, she asked him for ten dollars. The husband unfortunately has only nine dollars and in that case she says he will not receive from her complete satisfaction. However, after a period of caresses and embraces, he hears her murmuring to him:

"Darling, I will lend you the remaining dollar until tomorrow."

*

A husband is no longer able to satisfy the frequent amorous desires of his wife. He sees various doctors but they cannot help him. She advises him to consult a psychiatrist. The consultation is extremely successful.

He declines however to tell her what the treatment consists of. But she notices that every night before going to bed he locks himself up in the bathroom and stays there for a while. Curious, one evening, she peeps through the keyhole and listens intently. She sees him sitting on the enclosed toilet, holding his head between his hands and repeating to himself:

"She is not my wife. She is not my wife."

*

A father comes home and sees his little girl sitting on the doorstep with her head in her hands and looking very glum.

"What is the matter? Is something wrong?"

"Yes, there is! I just cannot get along with that wife of yours."

*

A man went to a pet store to buy a parrot. Of one the salesman said,

"He is a remarkable bird. If you pull his left leg, he will recite the Ten Commandments. If you pull his right leg, he will recite the Sermon on the Mount."

"Is that so? And what happens if I pull both legs?"

"You fool! I will fall from my perch!" replied the parrot.

*

Little boy to father:

"Daddy, what does the word vice mean?"

"Oh, it is a bad word. For example vice is when a husband cheats his wife or when a person drinks too much. Why do you ask?"

"It's because in school they have appointed me vice-president of my junior class fraternity."

*

To be bald in front means a great power to think. To be bald in the back is a sign of great virility.

What does it mean when a man is bald both in front and in the back?

It means that he thinks he is very virile.

*

A father scolds his little son for having brought home bad marks from school:

"Why can't you do as well as our neighbour's son who always brings back excellent marks?"

Little boy: "Well, he happens to be lucky: he has smart parents!"

*

An old lady bought a parrot to keep her company. To her great dismay, she later discovered that all the bird could say was,

"My name is Polly, I am a whore."

She didn't know what to do and talked about it to other people who owned parrots. Among them she found a lady who had two very religious parrots. They prayed all day, rolling prayer beads through their claws, so their owner had called them Mark and Luke. The first lady asked if she could put Polly with those two for a few days so that she might learn better language and it was so agreed. When Polly was put into the cage, the first thing she did was to introduce herself:

"My name is Polly, I am a whore."

Whereupon, Mark shouted joyfully to Luke,

"Throw your beads away, Luke! Our prayers have been answered."

*

A man bought a parrot at an auction after a spirited auctioning. "I suppose this bird talks," said the man to the auctioneer. "Talks?", replied the auctioneer." He has been bidding against you for the last half hour!"

*

A husband comes home unexpectedly and finds his wife in bed in the middle of the day. Next to her on the nighttable a cigar is burning in the ashtray.

Half out of his mind, he shouts at her,

"Where did this cigar come from?"

"I don't know. I must have been smoking it."

"If you don't tell me where this cigar is from, I will strangle you on the spot."

At that point a male voice can be heard from the inside of a closet,

"It comes from Havana."

*

A man who was in his high seventies had a young wife in her thirties. They went to see his doctor because they hadn't had any children.

The doctor advised him to take a roomer in their house.

A few weeks later, the two met on the street and the doctor asked,

"How is your wife?"

"Oh, she is wonderful. She is pregnant."

"I am glad to hear that. And how is your roomer?"

"Oh, she is pregnant too!"

*

An American pays a visit to his doctor because his hands continually tremble. The doctor inquires,

"Do you drink a lot?"

"Not too much. I spill most of it!"

*

A drunkard crawls around a lightpole in the middle of the night. A policeman asks him what he is doing.

"I am looking for my keys."

"Don't you remember where you have lost them?"

"Yes, over there near my house."

"Why, then, are you looking for them here instead of there?"

"Because here there is more light."

*

Towards the end of the day, Mary, one of the girls of a New York "house" took leave from the Madame.

"I will not come tomorrow. I feel sick."

"But you cannot do that to us! You are by far our best girl. I just tallied the business for today: you went upstairs 36 times!"

"Well, that's precisely it; my feet are killing me!"

*

In the US newly married couples no longer go on honeymoon trips: they save the money for their divorce.

*

Optimist: someone who believes that cars will cost 8000 dollars by 1990

Pessimist: someone who thinks that cars will cost 8000 rubles by 1990.

*

A boat sank in the middle of the ocean. Four people survived and floated for many days on a raft. Food ran out. As a result, the Englishman decided to sacrifice himself. He got up, saluted, shouted "Hail to the Queen," and jumped into the ocean. A day later his example was followed by the French who shouted "Vive la France."

A few days later as things had become totally desperate, the American got up, shouted "Hail America" and threw the Japanese into the water.

*

A Texas sheriff had not been reelected to his job. He had received only one vote from the entire village. The following morning he could be seen walking down main street wearing all his guns and ammunition.

A citizen stopped him and asked,

"Why are you wearing all this weaponry? You are no longer entitled to it. You are not sheriff anymore."

"My dear man, anyone who has as few friends in this town as I have better be armed to his teeth."

*

The apartment of a young New York model was broken into by a robber and the girl was raped.

The police asked her if she put up a fight with the robber.

"No, how could I? I had just painted my fingernails and the polish wasn't dry!"

*

The senior partner of a New York law firm came home from a golden anniversary wedding trip to Acapulco.

"How was it?" asked his friends.

"Oh, we went to the same hotel on the seashore, but there was one difference: this time *I* locked myself in the bathroom and cried!"

*

A woman tells her psychiatrist:

"Doctor, every night I have a most dreadful nightmare. I see myself walking in the streets all naked, wearing only a pair of shoes."

Doctor: "Aren't people looking at you?"

"Yes, and I don't mind a bit."

"So, what is the problem"

"The problem is that I am wearing my shoes from last year!"

*

An elderly gentleman comes to a brothel and wants to see Mary. But Mary isn't in and the Madame offers him a wide choice of other girls. But nothing will do. He insists on Mary and prefers to wait until she is back on the job. The Madame asks him what is so special about Mary, and the old gentleman answers:

"You see, Mary gives blue stamps and I need one more book to get a hairdryer for my wife on her birthday."

*

Three elderly ladies are having tea together. They discuss the careers and successes of their respective sons and compare the liberalities they receive from them.

First mother: "My son is just wonderful. He is so well off that each year he offers me a new car."

Second mother: "I cannot complain either. Knowing my passion for furcoats, my son offers me each Christmas one of the rarest and most expensive furcoats."

Third mother: "This is nothing compared with my son. He is spending every month more than a thousand dollars for talks with a psychiatrist and guess about whom they are talking?"

"Who?"

"Me!"

*

A girl who lives in a big American city wants to get her picture into the newspapers. She decides to follow the example of Lady Godiva, borrows a horse and rides naked in the center of town. She caused the greatest traffic jam ever known in that city, for the people had never seen a horse!

*

"I got elected!" shouted a US political candidate when he arrived home.

"I hope you are not lying," his wife replied.

"Certainly not. I don't have to anymore."

*

A visitor from England found the Americans to be very strange people.

"You order hot tea, then put ice in it to make it cold, then you put sugar in it to make it sweet, then you put lemon in it to make it sour, then you lift your glass and say "here's to you," and you drink it yourself!"

*

A little negro boy visits a priest and complains to him:

"Why did God make me black? Do you think it is fair?"

Priest: "Why don't you go to the church and tell it yourself to the Lord. I am sure he will hear you."

The boy goes, kneels in front of the altar and speaks to God:

"Why, O God, did you give me a black skin and not a white one, as you did for most people?"

God: "I wanted to be good to you. You must remember that your race lived in Africa. By giving you a black skin I protected you from the fierce rays of the sun."

"And why did you give me those ugly, curly short hair, while you gave to the white beautiful, soft, long hair?"

God: "Again, it was for your good. You had to run among the bushes to catch animals, and long hair would have entangled itself and impeded your run."

"Thank you very much. But why did you give me these flat,thickly soled feet?"

God: "Again, it was for your good. I did it so that you could better run and hunt while protecting your feet from cuts and bruises."

The little boy remains silent, reflects for a while and then addresses the Lord again:

"May I ask you a last question?"

"Yes, of course, dear boy."

"Well, if you really meant to be so good with me, why then was I born in Chicago?"

*

A black boy is tired of being black. One day he decides to paint his face white. When his father comes home and sees what he has done to himself, he gets mad and gives him a good spanking. The boy shouts back at him:

"I am white for only two hours, and already I can see what is to be expected from those damned niggers!"

*

American Indians have a prodigious memory. The story is told of two salesmen who were travelling on the same train and were commenting on the character and ways of American Indians. One said to the other:

"When you get off in Sioux Falls you will see an old Indian sitting at the station and sunning himself. You can ask him any question to test his memory."

When the salesman got off the train, he saw indeed the old Indian sitting there, and he asked him:

"When did you have eggs for breakfast for the first time in your life?"

"On 11 July 1923," answered the Indian.

A few years later the same salesman again travelled to Sioux Falls and when he saw the old Indian, his face lit up and he greeted the man cheerfully:

"How!"

And the Indian answered: "Scrambled."

*

Wisdom of an Indian chief:

"Four hundred years ago the red men were dwelling in America. There were no taxes, no national debt, no foreign wars, no nuclear arms, no pollution, no crime. How can the white man claim having made progress?"

*

An Indian chief was standing on a mountain making smoke signals when he saw the big mushroom cloud of an atomic explosion. He muttered: "I wish I had said that!"

*

An Indian chief was standing on top of a hill with his son, watching the beautiful valleys and landscape below them. He said to his boy,

"Someday, son, all this land will belong to the Indians again. Paleface all go to the moon."

*

Indian proverb:
Indian scalp enemies
White men skin friends

*

Cowboy to Indian:

"Can I leave my gun and my saddle in your tent?"

"Certainly. There is not a white man within 100 miles."

*

An Indian and a white man had been hunting all day long. They had strayed farther and farther away from the village. When the night came the white man said,

"I am afraid we are lost."

His companion answered,

"Indian not lost. Tepee lost."

*

Why do Indian women walk behind their men? In order to whisper to them the directions.

*

White man to Indian:

"How come you are using a chemical fire-extinguisher in your village?"

Indian: "I use it to correct my spelling mistakes when I make smoke signals."

*

Where are the fastest dogs in the world?
In Alaska, because the trees are so far apart.

*

A Texan visiting Vermont asks a local farmer:
"How large is your farm?"
"And how large is yours?"
"Well, it takes me about a full day to drive around it with my truck."
Vermonter: "I used to have a truck like that."

*

A Russian tourist visits the Grand Canyon and is told that it took five million years to carve out that canyon out of the rocks.
"I did not know that you had a State planning commission too!"

*

An American was showing a Russian an archaeological site where, deep in the Earth, they found a piece of copper wire. He said,
"This proves that in pre-historic times we had already telephone lines."
And the Russian said, "We have a similar site in the Soviet Union. In it we did not find any trace of wire. This proves that we had already wireless telegraph."

*

An American dairyman from Wisconsin visits Paris for the first time. He has dinner at a fine restaurant. Towards the end of the meal the waiter brings him a platter of cheeses on which he spots a beautiful camembert. He exclaims,
"I'll be damned! I didn't know that those Frenchmen made camembert too!"

*

The President of the United States wanted to send a US senator to an important world conference in Paris and asked,

"Do you know French?"

"Yes, a little. I have no trouble with waiters and taxi-drivers."

"Yes, but suppose there are no waiters and cab drivers at that conference?"

*

During an electoral campaign President Theodore Roosevelt was heckled by a listener who was shouting,

"I am a Democrat, I am a Democrat."

Roosevelt interrupted his speech and asked the man:

"And may I ask why you are a Democrat?"

"Because my grandfather and my father were Democrats."

"And suppose your grandfather and your father had been Republicans. What would you be today?"

"A jackass," replied the man.

*

President Reagan was to receive the President of France. In order to please the latter, he wanted to greet him with a few words of French. His assistants told him that he could greet him with the words "Bonjour, Monsieur le President." Reagan tried to learn these words by heart, but for safety purposes he wrote them down on a piece of paper which he pinned behind his necktie.

The following morning, when the President of France arrived, Reagan had forgotten the words, but he proudly remembered his foresight, flipped around his necktie and read from it these words,

"Pierre Cardin!"

*

An American requires a heart transfer. He is offered a choice between the heart of a 21-year-old tennis player, the heart of a 40-year-old golf player and that of an 85-year-old Republican politician. The man chose the latter. Asked why he had made that choice, he answered,

"His heart gives me the best chance to live because I know that it has never been used.

*

The President of the United States was furious because most of what was going on in the White House was known to the Russians. So he decided that the next top-secret meeting of the National Security Council would be held in the vault of the Bank of America. After a while the Secretary of Defense wanted to leave the vault to go to the bathroom, but the President retorted,

"Under no circumstances will anyone leave this room until our meeting is over." Whereupon a guard began knocking at the door from the outside asking that it be opened. Asked what he wanted the guard shouted through the door,

"Radio Moscow just announced that the Secretary of Defense needed to go to the bathroom."

*

The President of the United States arrives one morning late at the White House. He looks haggard and tired. His Secretary asks him:

"What is the matter with you?"

"Oh, it was awful. I had a terrible nightmare. I dreamt that I was attending the 38th Central Congress of the Communist Party, and President Brejnev was shouting at me because California had not fulfilled its target under the economic development plan."

"So what?"

"Well, it hurt me a lot, because I was the Secretary of the California State Communist Party!"

*

When President Reagan was asked if he was not too old to be President of the United States, he answered:

"In the Soviet Union I would not even be the minimum age to be eligible for the Polit Bureau!"

*

What is the difference between the three major American TV networks?

One is worse than the other.

*

During the height of the depression of the US steel industry, a big steel magnate died and arrived in heaven. He did not like it there and asked for a transfer to hell. After a week the devil sent him back to God with a note:

"You better keep him. He is a disaster to us. Within a week he has shut down five furnaces!"

*

President Carter died. When he arrived in heaven, St. Peter told him that he would have to wait a while until his file had been processed. In the meantime, he had asked President Theodore Roosevelt to keep him company. The latter asked Carter how things were on Earth.

"Not very good. For example, the Soviets have invaded Afghanistan."

"So you must be at war with them."

"No."

"So what are you doing?"

"We are boycotting the Olympic Games which are held in Moscow."

"And what else is there?"

"Well, the Iranians are holding three dozens of American hostages."

"So I assume that you are at war with Iran."

"No."

"Well, what then are you doing?"

"We asked Secretary-General Waldheim to mediate."

"What else is there, closer to home?"

"Things are not much better. For instance, Cuba has become communist."

"So I assume that you are at war with Cuba."

"No."

"So what are you doing?"

"We boycott their sugar exports."

"What else is there?"

"Nicaragua is also becoming communist."

"So I assume that we are at war with Nicaragua."

"No."

"What then are you doing?"

"We are arming El Salvador and Honduras."

At that moment, St. Peter comes back and takes Carter to his quarters in paradise. Teddy Roosevelt walks away, immersed in somber thoughts. Suddenly he exclaims,

"Am I glad that this son of a bitch died! If he had stayed alive I am sure he would have given away my Panama Canal!"

*

An Italian immigrant passing by a rich suburban mansion in Westchester County saw the owner sprawled in an armchair in front lawn. The Italian approached him.

"Sir, I have several children and no work. Would you by any chance have a little job for me to do?"

"Well, at least you are not begging and you want to work which is the true American spirit. Here is a can of white paint. Go to the back of the house and paint the porch. I'll pay you 200 dollars."

After a half hour the Italian reports to the owner that the job is finished.

"What! You painted that porch in half a hour?"

"It was a Mercedes-Benz, not a Porsche."